# POLE WORK

## for Dressage Riders

**Also by Ann Katrin Querbach**

*50 Best Arena Exercises and Patterns*

Ann Katrin Querbach

# POLE WORK
## for Dressage Riders

Translated by Karen Brittle and Anja Cain

Trafalgar Square
North Pomfret, Vermont

First published in the English language in 2023 by
Trafalgar Square Books
North Pomfret, Vermont 05053

Originally published in the German language as *Stangen Workout für Dressurreiter* by Müller Rüschlikon Verlag, Stuttgart

Copyright © 2020 Müller Rüschlikon Verlag, Stuttgart
English translation © 2023 Trafalgar Square Books

All rights reserved. No part of this book may be reproduced, by any means, without written permission of the publisher, except by a reviewer quoting brief excerpts for a review in a magazine, newspaper, or website.

**Disclaimer of Liability**
The author and publisher shall have neither liability nor responsibility to any person or entity with respect to any loss or damage caused or alleged to be caused directly or indirectly by the information contained in this book. While the book is as accurate as the author can make it, there may be errors, omissions, and inaccuracies.

Trafalgar Square Books encourages the use of approved safety helmets in all equestrian sports and activities.

ISBN: 978 1 64601 098 1
Library of Congress Control Number: 2022945138

Photographs by Sabine Kielmann except pp. 60, 61, 64, 69 (Ann Katrin Querbach); pp. 35, 47, 76, 82, 90, 91, 99 (Horst Streitferdt, www.foto-streitferdt.de); p. 17 (Berit Wolf); p. 165 (Jasmin Ziegler).

Diagrams by Dorothee Dumm

Design by www.ravenstein2.de
Cover design by RM Didier
Index by Andrea M. Jones (www.jonesliteraryservices.com)
Typefaces: Proxima Nova, Rotis Semi Sans

Printed in China

10 9 8 7 6 5 4 3 2 1

# CONTENTS

Introduction .................................................................................................... 1

## 1. Why Is Pole Work Good for Horses? ...................................................... 4
    1.1    An Overview of the Benefits ................................................................ 8
    1.2    When Should I Avoid Working with Poles? ..................................... 10
    1.3    What to Know Before Getting Started or Continuing Pole Work:
          When Do I Need a Trainer? ............................................................... 11

## 2. Exercises to Prepare and Correct ........................................................ 12
          **Side Note: The Correct Bend** ........................................................... 13
          **Side Note: Axial Alignment** ............................................................. 16
    2.1    Motivating the Horse .......................................................................... 19
    2.2    Unconventional but Effective ............................................................ 20
    2.3    A Square of Cones .............................................................................. 22
    2.4    Lifting the Leg with Correct Flexion ................................................. 24
    2.5    Perfecting the Canter Rhythm ........................................................... 25
          **Side Note: Positive Tension** ............................................................. 27

## 3. Walking Exercises with Poles ............................................................... 29
          **Side Note: Aids at the Walk** ............................................................ 32
          **Side Note: A Centered, Supple Position** ........................................ 35
    3.1    The Basic Setup .................................................................................. 37
    3.2    Adding More Poles ............................................................................. 38
    3.3    The Fan at the Walk ........................................................................... 39
    3.4    Raise It Up Correctly .......................................................................... 41
    3.5    The Raised Fan ................................................................................... 42

# CONTENTS

**4. Trot Work on the Longe** .................................................................................... 44
    4.1   Why Is Trotting Poles Good for Horses? ........................................... 47
          **Side Note: Are Side-Reins Helpful?** ................................................ 48
    4.2   Finding the Way ..................................................................................... 49
    4.3   Finding Rhythm ..................................................................................... 51
    4.4   A Light Workout .................................................................................... 53
    4.5   Abs, Legs, and Butt for Your Horse .................................................... 55
          **Side Note: Naturally Crooked or Nice and Straight?** .................... 56
          *Pole Workouts for Horses Who Fall In* ............................................. 57
          *Pole Workouts for Horses Who Fall Out* ......................................... 61
    4.6   The Endless Circle ................................................................................. 63
          **Extra: Abs, Legs, and Butt for Riders** ............................................. 66
          **A Short Case Study** ........................................................................... 68

**5. Trot Poles on Straight Lines** .............................................................................. 70
          **Side Note: The Aids at the Trot** ....................................................... 71
    5.1   The Trio .................................................................................................. 73
    5.2   A Line of Six .......................................................................................... 75
    5.3   The Long Line ....................................................................................... 77
    5.4   The Long Line with Angled Poles ...................................................... 79
    5.5   The Long Line, Raised .......................................................................... 81

**6. Trot Poles on Bending Lines** .............................................................................. 83
    6.1   The Quartet ........................................................................................... 84
    6.2   A Circle with Eight ............................................................................... 86
    6.3   The Quartet in a Row .......................................................................... 89
    6.4   High Up—Part 1 .................................................................................. 90
    6.5   High Up—Part 2 .................................................................................. 91

**7. Combinations** ........................................................................................................ 93
    7.1   Combo 1 ................................................................................................. 96
    7.2   Combo 2 with a Change of Direction ............................................... 97
    7.3   Improving Transitions and Rhythm ................................................ 100
    7.4   Side and High ..................................................................................... 101
    7.5   Every Which Way ............................................................................... 102
          **Side Note: Posting Trot Correctly** ................................................ 104
          **Side Note: Half-Halts and Full Halts** ........................................... 107

# CONTENTS

| | | |
|---|---|---|
| 7.6 | The Simple Serpentine | 108 |
| 7.7 | Change across the Long Diagonal | 109 |
| 7.8 | Serpentines | 110 |
| 7.9 | Infinity Loop | 111 |
| 7.10 | Figure Eight | 112 |

**8. Canter Exercises on the Longe** ............................................................ 114
- 8.1 How to Begin .................................................................................. 118
- 8.2 Tempo and Rhythm ........................................................................ 120
- 8.3 Double In-Out ................................................................................ 121
- 8.4 Canter Workout .............................................................................. 124
- 8.5 Cavalletti in Gradual Stages .......................................................... 125

**9. Canter Poles on Bending Lines** ............................................................ 127
- Side Note: Canter Aids on Bending Lines ........................................ 130
- 9.1 The Canter Square ......................................................................... 130
- 9.2 The Canter Quartet ........................................................................ 132
- 9.3 Abs, Legs, Butt .............................................................................. 134
- 9.4 Interplay ........................................................................................ 136
- 9.5 Infinity Loop at Canter ................................................................... 138

**10. Canter Poles on Straight Lines** ........................................................... 140
- 10.1 The Canter Trio ............................................................................. 141
- 10.2 The Canter Sextet ........................................................................ 143
- 10.3 The Long Line of Poles at Canter ................................................. 144
- 10.4 The Long Line of Poles, Raised .................................................... 146
- 10.5 The Raised Diagonal .................................................................... 147

**11. Changes in Tempo** ................................................................................ 149
- 11.1 Lengthening the Stride ................................................................. 151
- 11.2 Shortening the Trot on a Bending Line ........................................ 154
- 11.3 Lengthening the Trot .................................................................... 156
- 11.4 Collecting the Trot ....................................................................... 158
- 11.5 Changing the Trot Tempo across the Diagonal ........................... 161

**Acknowledgments** ..................................................................................... 167
**Index** ........................................................................................................... 169

# INTRODUCTION

# Introduction

For every rider, the health of the horse should be a top priority. Yet all too often, you'll see horses who are being ridden in ways that work against their natural way of going. Performance for sport or work most often takes top priority—in my opinion, this should be secondary to the horse's general health and well-being. Unfortunately, the same holds true for pleasure riders: horses are often asked to work at the expense of their own well-being, despite the fact that many pleasure riders do consider their horse's care a central priority. It's here that we often encounter a crucial misunderstanding: "care" isn't the same as actually keeping the horse healthy! Pleasure riders, for the most part, have lost track of the traditional classical training for their horses—a phenomenon that has had broad implications for the health and soundness of their horses.

At major competitions, you will not only see horses who don't use their backs at all, you'll also frequently see very, very tense horses. Thank God this isn't always the case! Horses that travel correctly over their backs are once again becoming a more common sight. However, among pleasure riders, it's usually possible to recognize clear deficits in the training of horse and rider. Basic elements of training, such as coordination, strength, and endurance, are often sadly lacking. Unfortunately, the result is that our dear and reliable equine partners lack positive tension in their bodies. In addition, training is often confused with a dominating approach and/or physical conditioning. Teaching commands can be important in emergency situations or when a serious disobedience occurs, but this won't be necessary most of the time, if the training is correct. Additionally, teaching commands and conditioning the horse to blindly follow doesn't have anything to do with healthy development of the muscles.

Riding, regardless of your discipline, is not easy, and requires years of daily practice and reflection. In this book, I'd like to not only offer you a variety of exercises you can apply to daily training, but also support you in your reflection and analysis as it relates to your horse and your own riding ability. Since 2007, I've been guiding horses and riders in their training, including overall development and correcting training issues. I've also supported my clients and their horses during illnesses or rehabilitation after injury. In many cases, we're presented with a problem only to find it is the result of poor riding. With the help of these exercises, it is possible to ride the horse correctly and avoid detrimental effects of bad riding.

I hope you'll find these various exercises motivating, fun, and a pleasure to undertake with your horse. You'll gain new knowledge, which you can apply to help keep your horse healthy and sound into old age!

# 1. WHY IS POLE WORK GOOD FOR HORSES?

Working over ground poles is a familiar concept to most riders. Likewise, riders are also often aware it's good for their horses, maybe as a way to improve rhythm. That's great! But in that case, which exercises actually improve the horse's rhythm? And what's the best sequence in which to do these exercises, in order for them to be most effective? In this book, I'll explain how you can best use the many different options for pole work with your horse, allowing you to train systematically.

But first I'd like to provide an overview of the advantages that gymnastic exercises with ground poles can offer. For many horses, it's difficult to maintain an even tempo over a longer period of time. Working over poles is a way to both improve and check up on the horse's rhythm. This work develops coordination, balance, and concentration for both horse and rider. At the same time, the rider develops a feel for the correct trot, active hindquarters, and lifted back. The rider learns to maintain a "positive tension" (also referred to as "tone" or "engagement") in her body, even as she stays loose enough to follow the horse's movement.

The hindquarters are active, as the horse must lift his hind legs significantly higher than usual in order to clear the poles, and the coordination of the dorsal and ventral muscle chains is thereby developed. This causes the horse to lift his back and engage the nuchal ligament of his neck. How can a horse build muscles in a manner that's both systematic and correct? That's exactly what I'll explain in the following pages! The exercises are presented in such a way that they logically follow one another. In addition, you'll always find further exercises ("Side Notes") on specific topics, which include suggestions that can be especially beneficial.

First, let's clarify a few terms and concepts.

## A Short Explanation about Muscle Chains

Skeletal muscles function via muscle chains. These chains connect different regions of the body with one another and allow the horse to move. The dorsal and ventral muscle chains are the most well-known—they work antagonistically (against one another).

### The Dorsal Muscle Chain

When describing the horse's dorsal muscles, we are referring to those that run along his back. These begin with the muscles of the upper neck, followed by the ligament system of neck and back, and then the muscles of the back, loin, and croup. Other important muscles are the hamstrings, which are part of the dorsal chain.

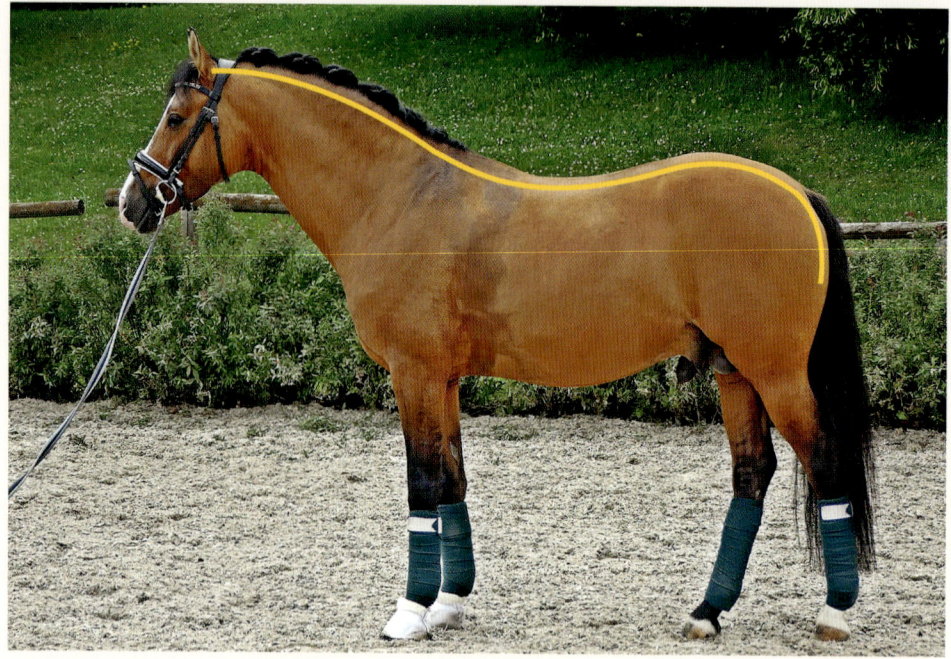

A simple design—the dorsal muscle chain runs from the upper neck muscles, over the neck and back, all the way to the posterior thigh muscles.

The ventral muscle chain runs along the bottom of the neck, over the abdominals, and all the way to the frontal thigh muscles.

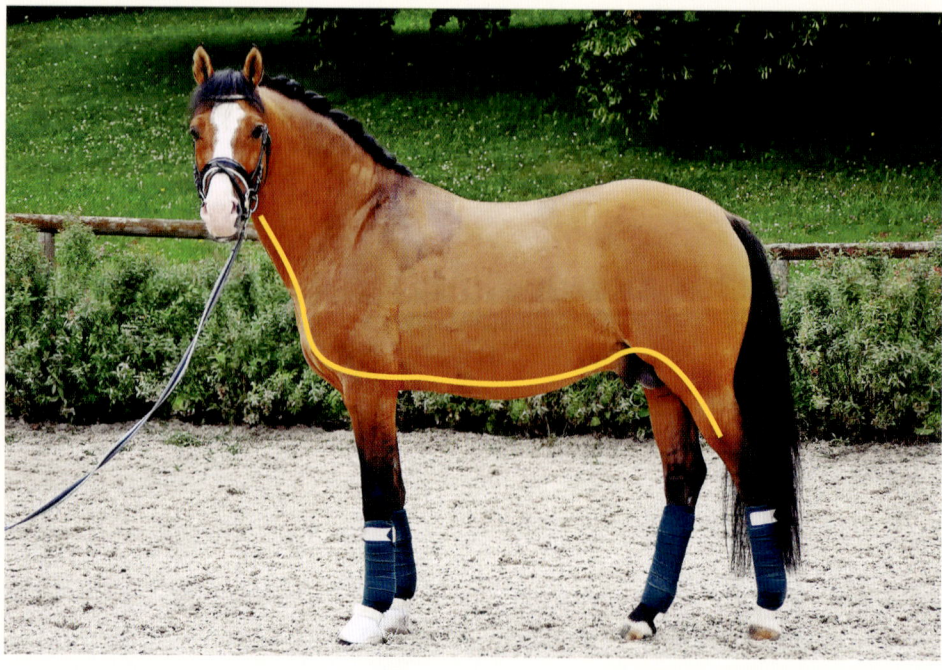

## The Ventral Muscle Chain

This runs along the ventral (belly) side of the horse. This includes the lower muscles of the neck, the abdominals, the flexors of the transition between the thoracic spine and the lumbar spine, the flexors of the lumbo-sacral joint, and the front thigh muscle.

The ventral muscle chain of the neck works closely with the abdominal (belly) muscle chain; in this way, they both strengthen each other. The abdominal muscle chain is composed of multiple muscular layers, which cross over one another on multiple levels. These run from the breastbone over the ribs, all the way back to the pelvic and groin area.

Unless these muscle chains are all worked correctly, the horse doesn't stand a chance of developing the carrying ability and "pushing power" he needs—this results in the false development of his muscles to compensate for their incorrect usage.

What does that mean, exactly? Instead of the correct muscle chains developing, individual muscles take over the work for those that are too weak, just to get through the daily movement required. This might originate with incorrect riding, or because of blockages and tension in the body. If these blockages and incorrect muscular development remain factors for too long, it will have a negative effect on tendons and ligaments, which can lead to inflammation and tears (the dreaded soft tissue injury).

Therefore, I urge you to pay careful attention to the correct muscular development of your horse. If you're not sure that your horse is developing correctly, you can seek the advice of a veterinarian, physiotherapist, or qualified body worker.

And with the use of pole work, you can check in to make sure your horse is using the correct muscles and demonstrating correct movement patterns.

To move correctly, the horse needs good coordination between his hindquarters and forehand.

# First, Let's Look at the Two Sources of Movement

**The forehand** consists of three active muscle chains: the trunk (responsible for lifting the breastbone); the upper neck; and the straight abdominal muscle. These three muscle chains work together to carry forward the movement and energy generated by the hindquarters. The forehand must be actively engaged in order to avoid damage to the legs or back.

**The hindquarters** consist of the croup muscles, the straight and transverse abdominal muscles, and the interior lumbar (loin) muscles. It's only possible for the horse to track up actively and carry weight correctly when his pelvis is able to rotate back and down.

The diaphragm binds these two central sources of movement together. Therefore, the horse must engage his body in a state of positive tension in order for him to be able to live a healthy and pain-free life.

# 1.1 An Overview of the Benefits

- Improve the dorsal and ventral muscle chains
- Synchronize the forehand with the hindquarters
- Improve rhythm, suppleness, connection
- Develop concentration, coordination, and conditioning
- Activate the hind end
- Strengthen the exterior muscle loop of the hindquarters
- Strengthen the shoulder girdle and the pelvic girdle
- Lift the breastbone (thus lightening the forehand)
- Create deeper flexion in the joints of the hindlegs
- Build and increase engagement of the topline

1. Why Is Pole Work Good for Horses?

Work over ground poles improves abdominal muscle tone.

In this photo, activation of the hindquarters through ground pole work is clearly visible.

Here, the activation of the hindquarters has visibly allowed the forehand to lift.

- Improve straightness
- Improve throughness
- Improve both carrying power and "pushing power"
- Improve tempo changes within the gaits

Working over poles will only have positive effects when the horse is guided to move correctly.

➡ **Working over ground poles is strenuous for the horse; therefore, you should limit your sessions to 15 minutes or less at a time.**

## 1.2 When Should I Avoid Working with Poles?

- After an injury, tendon damage, or when a horse is in rehabilitation after an operation, it's important to first consult with your veterinarian.
- When the horse has a physical block, it should first be treated fully by a chiropractor, osteopath, or physiotherapist.

- When the horse suffers from chronic ailments of the hoof or legs, you should seek veterinary advice before doing this work.
- Finally, if a horse has an incorrect or uneven way of going, working over poles may do more harm than good. That's why it's important that basic correct use of both the hindquarters and forehand be established first.

## 1.3 What to Know Before Getting Started or Continuing Pole Work: When Do I Need a Trainer?

- The horse is behind or above the bit during training
- There's no musculature at the base of the neck
- The horse has a weak trapezius muscle that isn't improving with training
- There is false bend in the neck
- There is stiffness of the poll
- There is muscle wasting along the spine/loins
- There are fatty deposits along the loin
- The horse has a short, choppy walk stride
- The horse shows four-beating at the canter that isn't improving with training
- The horse is hanging on your hands
- The horse is twisting at the poll (frequently or in specific situations)

➡ *So long as the horse isn't dealing with a physiological block, working over poles has the potential to improve these faulty patterns of movement. However, if applied incorrectly, these exercises can also make things worse.*

If you notice your horse exhibiting any of these behaviors during your training, you should immediately enlist an expert to advise you.

➡ *Make sure you regularly check your saddle fit! Working over poles can have a positive influence on the horse's physical development. As a result, a saddle that fits well when you're just beginning can become too tight over time.*

# 2. EXERCISES TO PREPARE AND CORRECT

## 2. Exercises to Prepare and Correct

Before we get started with pole work, you can begin by practicing the five exercises from this chapter. These exercises will also be useful if you encounter problems with pole work, as they can be used as corrective exercises.

First, we want to develop the horse's motivation for pole work. With the following exercises, you'll help the horse improve his rhythm and balance, as well as his ability to bend in the walk and trot. You'll also find an exercise specifically for canter, which prioritizes rhythm and balance as well.

If your horse is already familiar with pole work, can bend confidently and correctly, and will stay on the aids at the canter, you can confidently skip this chapter and begin instead with chapter 3.

However, make sure you don't skip the exercises below ("The Correct Bend"). It might prove interesting for you.

Take this book with you when you ride. My suggestion is that you keep it somewhere close at hand, along the rail. When you encounter a problem, you can immediately look up a relevant corrective exercise and go ride it.

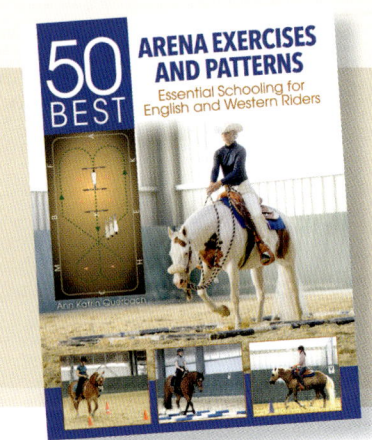

In my previous book, *50 Best Arena Exercises and Patterns: Essential Schooling for English and Western Riders*, you can find many more exercises that may also be helpful for problem-solving issues with your horse.

## SIDE NOTE: THE CORRECT BEND

The advice that "the horse should bend around your inside leg" is often misunderstood: riders apply a strong pressure with the inside leg, apply the inside rein with excessive force to "position" the horse, and at the same time allow their outside hand to come forward incorrectly, as if riding a bicycle.

Of course, these issues might not be as extreme as described with most riders, but the following exercise doesn't just focus on bending in an interesting way—it will deepen the rider's knowledge of her horse's biomechanics and her ability to maintain her own seat correctly throughout the bend. This is often eye-opening and improves the rider's ability to analyze what's happening.

Bending correctly, for a horse, requires an appropriate amount of muscular stability from both the forehand and the hindquarters.

Therefore, a correct bend begins with the control and stabilization of the outside shoulder and pelvic girdle during the stance phase.

A "twist" via the inside rein should always be avoided. Horses' reactions to a too-tight rein are always detrimental to their overall soundness.

A correctly bending horse steps with his hind leg in the track of his foreleg, takes the carrying load onto an active inside hind leg, and has enough freedom through the shoulder to bring his inside foreleg forward. The three axes (leg, chest, and head) are aligned. This can only take place if the musculature along the horse's outside is engaged.

This goal evolves from good and purposeful training, which requires responsibility, self-discipline, and self-reflection.

The horse can be the rider's mirror, not only in terms of her mental condition, but also physically. The central axis of the horse's breastbone and the central axis of the rider's upper body should always be aligned and parallel. The same applies to the axes of the rider's legs and the horse's legs.

In order for the horse to be ridden correctly and therefore stay sound, the horse must bend correctly. Correct bending, in turn, requires sufficient stability in the outside muscles on the bending line.

## How Can This Theoretical Knowledge Carry Over into Practice?

### Let's Begin with the Rider's Seat

To put it simply: during a bending movement, the space from the horse's shoulder to his hip is shorter on the inside than the outside. To encourage the horse to contract his inner back muscles, the rider should put weight on her inside seatbone.

To do so, the rider holds her inner torso (hip to shoulder) stable and brings her inside shoulder just a little forward. Here, we're talking about just a millimeter—and it's also different for each horse and rider combination. You're going to find the right position for your shoulder by exploring the following exercises.

### Exercise 1:

Imagine you're carrying a heavy sack of flour on your inside shoulder, and you don't want it to fall. If you fold your inner hip and allow your inner shoulder to drop, your flour sack will fall.

## Exercise 2:

1. Have a friend sit comfortably on a chair or bench. Then sit on your friend's knees.
2. Applying the degree of torso stability described above, put weight on your seat bone on your left side.
3. Now, have your friend pull her right knee out from under you.
4. If you're seated with true stability, you will correctly stabilize your body over your left seat bone. However, if you lose your balance when your friend pulls her right knee away, you weren't sitting in the correct position for riding a left bend on your horse.

Repeat this exercise more than once to develop the correct feel. Horses that don't want to contract their inner back muscles through a bend will cause the rider to sit to the outside. Often, the saddle will slip to the outside as a result.

Let's stay with the rider's aids on the inside of the bending horse. Because the rider's inside shoulder is coming forward just the slightest bit, her inside hand can also make room for the horse's inside shoulder to step forward. In this way, the rider can establish a light connection with the horse's mouth, without over-positioning the horse to the inside.

➡ ***The bend doesn't begin through positioning with the reins, but rather in the horse's body.***

The rider's inside leg has the job of animating and helping the horse's inside hind leg as it steps forward. In addition, the rider's inside leg adjusts the forehand to the hindquarters, which helps to lengthen the rider's torso on the inside.

➡ ***The rider must remain stable on the side of the horse that is in the direction of the bend.***

The rider's outside aids are important when asking the horse to bend. When we're riding a bending line, we must *think diagonally.* This means the consistent presence of both a stable inside hip (not gripping, but stable) and steady outside rein. This allows the rider to support the horse's outside shoulder against the centrifugal force generated by the bend, which provides stability in the shoulder girdle and thereby prevents a twisting of the horse's chest. I'm not talking about a tight rein—rather a stable and limiting rein that maintains a soft, steady connection with the horse's mouth.

Through this diagonal stability on the part of the rider, the horse receives the aids that he needs in order to develop his lateral musculature and the synchronization of forehand and hindquarters. Now, the horse's inside hind end will take over and provide energy, rather than the outer shoulder girdle.

The rider's outside leg regulates the outside of the horse. In doing so, it helps to improve axial alignment—that is, the positioning of the forehand in relation to the hindquarters.

➡ *The more theoretical knowledge we can learn and apply to analyzing and improving our position, the better we'll ride.*

But don't start to think this is all going to be too complicated for you. Riding isn't just a technical undertaking, it's a combination of feel, timing, knowledge, technique, and refined communication. We riders have a demanding task: to train our equine partners, to support them, to help them, and to develop them using correct techniques that keep them sound and motivated.

## SIDE NOTE: AXIAL ALIGNMENT

By now, you must be wondering whether math has suddenly become important for riding. No, this book actually isn't very mathematical. But axial alignment is indeed an important aspect of equitation, and should absolutely be regarded as basic knowledge for riding horses with long-term soundness as a goal.

When referring to axial alignment, we're primarily visualizing three distinct lines. (Take note: here, I'm only describing the three lines that one can see from the front.)

1. The line from poll to nose
2. The chest axis
3. The leg axis (chest to hoof)

These three lines should always present as parallel to one another and vertical to the ground. Every rider has had these lines fall out of alignment. Some examples might include:

➡ A crooked poll
➡ A horse that leans around a turn like a motorcycle
➡ A tendon strain or tear, or a stressed limb

## 2. Exercises to Prepare and Correct

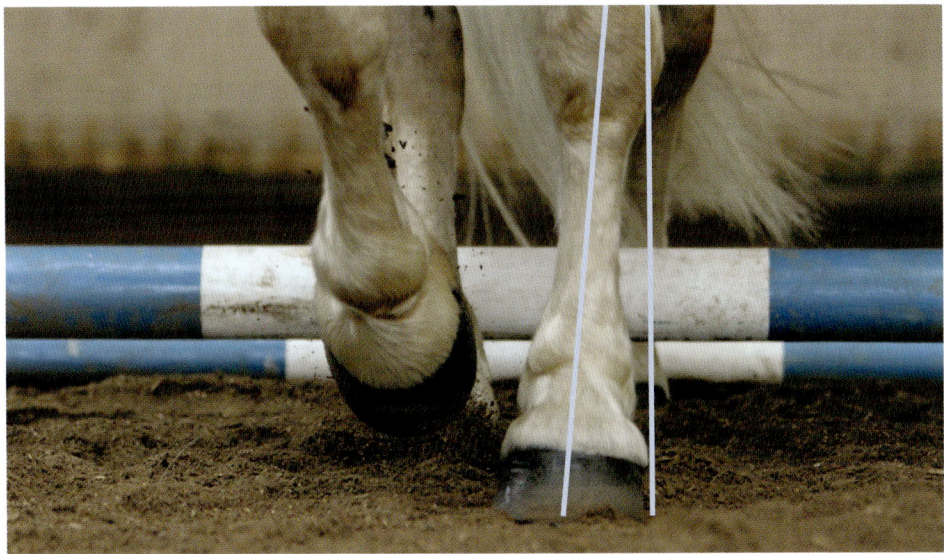

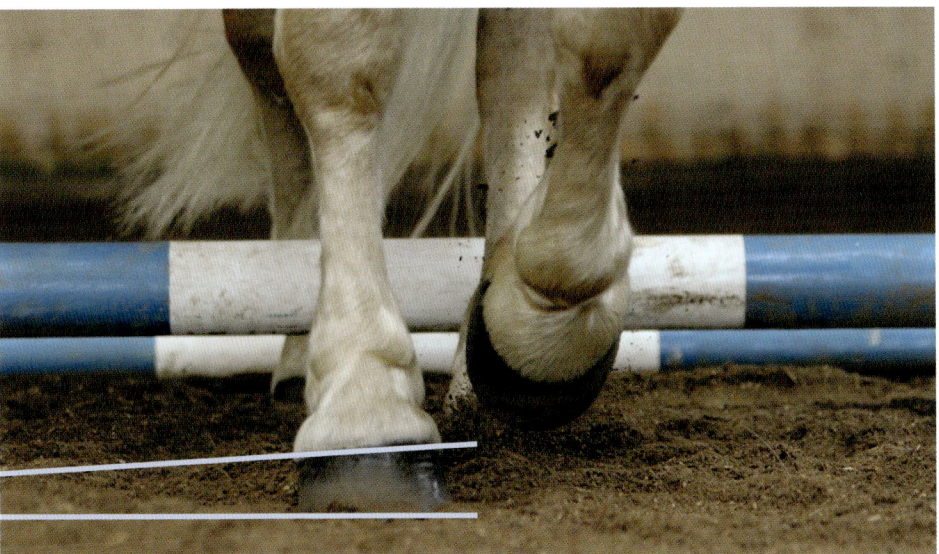

In both pictures, something is recognizably amiss in the axial alignment of the forelegs. The feet are landing too close to one another (base narrow), which can easily be confirmed by the visibly sloped coronet band.

---

With all of these examples, there is or was an axial misalignment.

To ride your horse for continued soundness or to help other riders do so, it's important to understand axial alignment. It's also important for instructors and trainers to develop an eye for this.

As an example: if the horse is crooked at the poll, the axis between his poll and neck is lopsided (off the vertical). It's no longer in alignment with the leg axes (chest to hoof). If the crookedness is the result of a too-strong inside rein, it will normally resolve itself when the inside rein is released so the horse connects clearly with the outside rein instead of the inside. This should correct the line from poll to nose, and the other axes will also become aligned.

If it's not the inside rein that's to blame, but rather the horse has gone through his training over time with his poll in this misaligned position, you will need an expert to advise you. Your expert should be someone who can encourage the horse to release the tension or block that has developed. If you look at the horse from the front, the axes from poll to nose, chest to legs, and the chest itself (neck to chest) should all be aligned with one another vertically.

If the nose and chest line are turned to the outside, this will result in a crooked breastbone. In this case, the outside shoulder girdle will not be stable enough to counteract gravity or centrifugal forces.

➡ *A crooked poll always signifies that the breastbone is twisted.*

If the nose and chest axis align—and are also perpendicular to the ground—but the leg axes present as crooked, this indicates a tense or heavy forehand. In this case, the horse's way of going should be looked at carefully again, and if necessary, he should be examined by an experienced bodyworker.

In such cases, you'll hear people say the horse "falls onto his shoulders." This is also noticeable when the horse's hooves wear unevenly. The source of the problem is that the inside shoulder cannot move upward freely when bending or turning; instead, the inside foreleg stays standing, turns laterally, and crosses with the outside shoulder. Only once axial alignment is achieved can the horse be considered sound again for riding purposes. Crooked axes are a sign that the horse is not stabilizing correctly and can no longer work against gravity via positive tension in his body.

The moment that his leg axis is not perpendicular to the ground, but instead even slightly crooked, his tendons and ligaments are being overburdened. This overburdening can lead to pain, lameness, inflammation of the tendon and its sheath, and tendon injuries. To maintain a sound horse, the rider, riding instructor, and trimmer or farrier must work together to realign the horse along this axis. You can't achieve this on your own, but working together can make it possible for the horse to have a long, sound life. If the horse presents with physical tension, bring an expert bodyworker into the mix. If a weak

# 2. Exercises to Prepare and Correct

forehand or hind end is to blame, pole work can also have good results in terms of re-establishing stability.

You want to ensure your horse also has fun with pole work and doesn't just associate it with sweat and hard training. You want him to be motivated and "ears forward" as he approaches his training with joy. In order to help ensure this, I have a small exercise for you and your horse: "Motivating the Horse for Pole Work."

## 2.1 Motivating the Horse

*In order for your horse to learn that he shouldn't hit the poles as he crosses over, place one pole in the middle of the arena.*

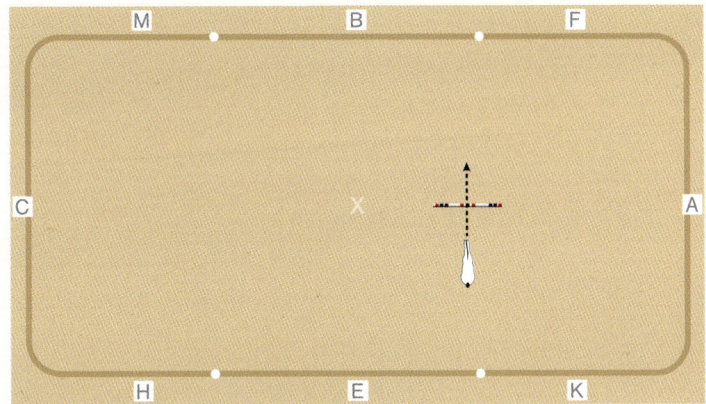

➡ **With horses who are somewhat "resistant to learning," ride a volte with the hindquarters placed to the outside before repeating the exercise. This will activate the hindquarters and develop attention span. Avoid the overuse of spurs or whip, and be patient.**

At the trot, ride over the ground pole, and don't allow your reins to interfere with the horse's movement. Keep your hips relaxed and swinging, so you don't block the horse. Sit tall and look through your horse's ears toward the arena rail.

If your horse travels over the pole without hitting it, stop and give him lots of praise. If your horse hits the pole, repeat the exercise until he doesn't hit it. (Always in moderation, of course.)

Stop the training session when the horse has gone over the pole without hitting it. This way, he gets the opportunity to go back to his stall or pasture while he's feeling great. You'll see that the next time, he'll already do the exercise better and quicker. Give your horse time to learn!

## Solutions to Common Problems

**"My horse always hits the pole, and he doesn't care."**
**"I'm losing my patience!"**
- Read over the section "How Horses Learn" in my book *50 Best Arena Exercises and Patterns: Essential Schooling for English and Western Riders*. Take three deep breaths and entertain a positive thought. Your horse will only learn if you're a calm and fair teacher.
- Horses only hit the poles when they have faulty musculature—for example, your horse will hit the pole if he's heavy on the forehand, or doesn't have an active hind end. This will change through training over ground poles. Begin with trot poles on a straight line.
- Many horses no longer hit the poles when they're motivated by lavish praise.
- With nervous horses, I recommend you start with an "alley" of poles and allow your horse to follow an experienced lead horse through the exercise.

**"I do this exercise on the longe, and my horse understands what I'm asking for just fine. But then when I try to ride the exercise, he hits the poles again."**
- The most likely culprit is a block in the rider's body or an incorrect seat. My best advice is that you speak with your physiotherapist, osteopath, or bodyworker.

**Your Horse Has Mastered This Exercise—What's Next?**
- If you used this exercise as preparation, you can now move on to the other exercises in this chapter.
- If you used this as a corrective exercise, you can go back to the exercises you were last working on.

# 2.2 Unconventional but Effective

*Although you might have the impression that the horse is moving rhythmically, his muscle chains cannot be working correctly unless his hindquarters are active. In order to train for this and recognize it while you're riding, the following exercise can be really helpful—whether accompanied by pole work or not.*

## 2. Exercises to Prepare and Correct

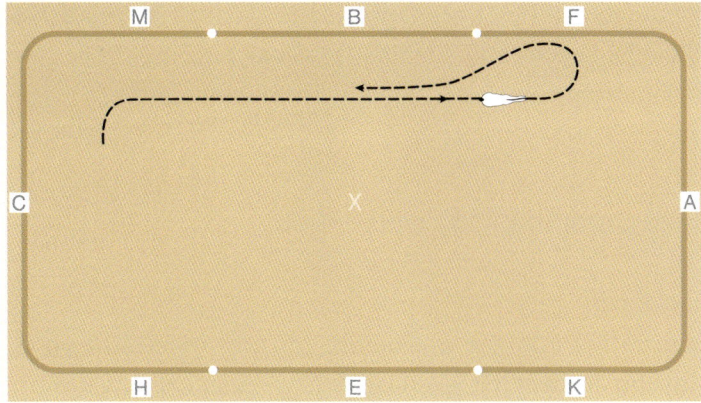

➡ **Don't help your horse too much; just ride a correct half circle to reverse direction toward the arena rail. Let your horse learn and recognize that his hindquarters were not correct before the turning point, and that you're not going to "babysit" him.**

Ride along the third track in trot. Let your horse trot on a loose rein. As soon as he loses rhythm or drifts to the outside or inside (i.e. falls onto his shoulder), turn him to the outside. Ride a half circle to reverse to the outside

After the turn, the hindquarters are active and the forehand lifts. This improves the horse's rhythm and throughness.

and then return to the third track. Now you're tracking in a new direction.

During the half circle, pay attention to make sure you drive clearly from your inside leg and position the horse with an opening rein.

---

### Solutions to Common Problems

**"My horse stops at the wall."**
- Ride a little further from the wall before you turn. Make sure you're applying your inside leg. Repeat this exercise until you can execute it with consistent rhythm both on the straightaway and through the half circle.

**"My horse picks up the canter."**
- Quietly transition your horse back down to the trot and repeat the exercise. Most likely, your horse had an underactive hind end before the half circle and wants to canter in order to gain impulsion.
- Check your leg position. If your outside leg came back too far, you unintentionally asked him to canter.

---

**Your Horse Has Mastered This Exercise—What's Next?**
➡ If you used this exercise as a warm-up, you can now go on to the other exercises in this chapter.
➡ If you used this as a corrective exercise, you can now go back to the previous exercises and try them again.

## 2.3 A Square of Cones

*Position 4 cones on a circle, evenly spaced around—they should form a square. This exercise improves steering and helps lift the horse's forehand. This exercise combines well with Exercise 7.5 (Stop Sign) in the book* 50 Best Arena Exercises and Patterns: Essential Schooling for English and Western Riders.

➡ **Be mindful! Keep your inner shoulder lifted (both shoulders should stay on the same line) so you don't collapse your inside hip and thereby give your horse a faulty weight aid.**

## 2. Exercises to Prepare and Correct

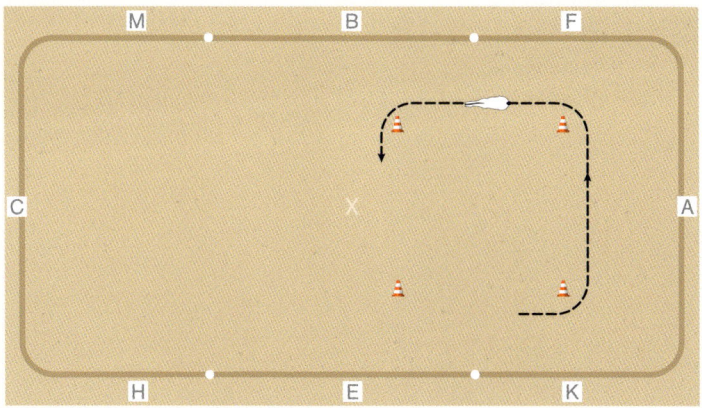

Ride a circle around the cones—tracking left, let's say. At each cone, turn your horse 90 degrees to the left. Support your horse using your outside leg, so that he stays on the aids and turns his forehand quickly. As this takes place, the hind legs must not be allowed to stop moving; if necessary, you should use your inside leg to activate the hindquarters.

### Solutions to Common Problems

**"My horse constantly runs over the cones..."**
- Is it possible that you've positioned the cones too close together? Spread them apart a bit.

**"My horse doesn't turn very quickly... instead it's almost like he's doing a volte...."**
- Drive more from your outside leg and keep your outside rein, making it easier for the horse to turn his forehand.

**Your Horse Has Mastered This Exercise—What's Next?**
- ➡ If you used this exercise as a warm-up, I recommend you move on to Exercise 2.4 (on the next page), or move on to the next chapter.
- ➡ If you used this as a corrective exercise, use the Table of Contents to quickly get you back to your prior exercise.

# 2.4 Lifting the Leg with Correct Flexion

*In order to make sure your horse is using the correct muscles—that is, he's not crooked—place two poles with one end lifted on a volte. Now ride over these in the walk.*

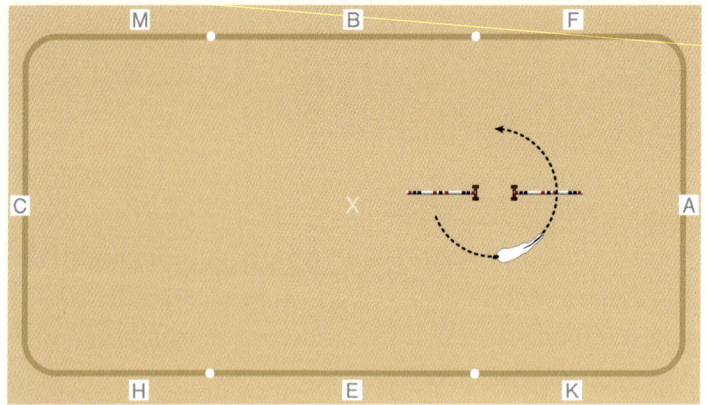

➡ **Don't steer as you travel over the poles; just guide and frame your horse over them.**

Continue to ride on the volte over the raised poles until your horse bends correctly and walks over the poles without hitting them.

As you do so, make sure you frame your horse well but don't block him. He should be learning to complete the exercise while maintaining positive tension in his body.

## Solutions to Common Problems

**"My horse falls to the outside."**
- This happens with most horses. Use your outside rein to limit your horse. Think about it this way: don't steer over the poles, just in between them—when all four legs have stepped over the pole.
  
  You can also use cones to mark the outside of the volte.

2. Exercises to Prepare and Correct

**Your Horse Has Mastered This Exercise—What's Next?**
You have many options about how to continue training from here:
- Work at the canter and practice the next exercise in this chapter.
- Move on to the walk exercises in the next chapter.
- Do some longeing work using the info in chapter 4.
- Try this exercise at the trot, and see what you can find in chapter 5 to help with this.
- If you used this as a corrective exercise, you can also check out the Table of Contents to quickly go back to whatever exercise you were previously attempting.

# 2.5 Perfecting the Canter Rhythm

*Place 4 cones on a bending line, with each one about 9–10 feet (3 meters) away from the next. Ride along the outside of the cones, as closely as possible, and count the number of canter strides that occur between the first and fourth cone.*

➡ ***Turn to page 128 to find info about the rider's aids for cantering on a bending line.***

In order to shorten the canter strides, the horse must get rounder and canter more clearly over his back. To help him achieve this, drive him toward the reins until you notice his back lifting and the canter strides getting shorter. For more information on how to do this, read about rider aids for canter on page 136.

Each time you round the circle, you should be able to get approximately four canter strides in between the four cones.

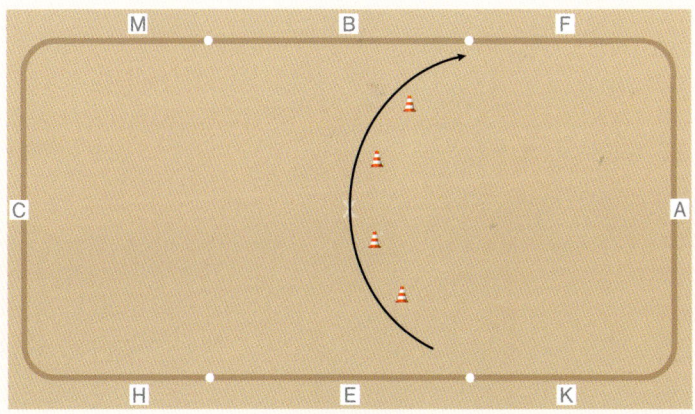

25

> ### Solutions to Common Problems
>
> **"It's difficult for me to count and ride at the same time…"**
> - Recruit an assistant to help in the arena and ask them to count for you.
>
> **"The circle gets so big that I'm no longer riding closely along the cones as my horse drifts to the outside."**
> - Position four additional cones in the arena to create four small gates to canter through. This way, you and your horse have a visual aid to help.

**Your Horse Has Mastered This Exercise—What's Next?**
   You have a lot of options for where to go from here:
   ⇒ Continue to work at the canter by turning to the exercises in chapter 9.
   ⇒ Work at the walk—see the next chapter.
   ⇒ Do some work on the longe, as described in chapter 4.
   ⇒ If you used this as a corrective exercise, go right back to whatever exercise you were doing beforehand.

With the application of the outside rein, the horse's standing leg phase will get longer, and the driving inside leg will encourage the horse to achieve a fluid, uphill canter.

# SIDE NOTE: POSITIVE TENSION

When developing and training horses, the concept of *losgelassenheit,* often translated as "relaxation" in English, is front and center. However, the term *losgelassenheit* does not really imply a "loose" or "lazy" relaxation; rather, it's referring to a horse that is supple and being ridden with positive tension.

*Losgelassenheit* implies an active springiness, which ideally is visible in the horse's swinging back. To accomplish this, the horse must absorb his own weight and the rider's weight, against the pull of gravity, and transform that weight into a newly invigorated movement. For this to work, there must be correct cooperation between his hindquarters, as motor, and his forehand, as "balanced steering system." The forehand—or, more accurately, the chest—can lift and lower.

This horse demonstrates positive tension, even at the halt.

We recognize when a horse has a lifted chest, or a sinking one, which we then describe as the horse "falling on his shoulders."

When the chest lifts, the nuchal ligament stretches, and the neck and head lower. However, if the forehand is passively sinking, the neck will still stretch forwards and downwards, but the shoulders can't lift up. If the horse has to step over a pole or uneven ground, the lower neck musculature will compensate. You can recognize this when the horse suddenly lifts his neck during a transition, or as soon as you start training over poles, or when he senses "danger." The back sinks and the horse braces.

In contrast, when positive tension is present, you will have a lifted forehand without the same kind of strain and bracing tension. When, as described previously, the musculature of the neck must help lift the forehand, there will always be bracing. In this case, too, when the forehand does lower, then the musculature no longer has positive tension, and the horse will become flaccid and run into the ground.

The hindquarters can rotate toward the head or the tail. We refer to the horse "tucking under" and tracking up actively when the hindquarters rotate toward the tail. In contrast, if the hindquarters rotate toward the head, the horse's back will sink and there will be a block in the lumbar region of the spine as well as in the lumbosacral joint.

Through correct pelvic rotation, the horse's center of movement can develop positive tension that works against gravity. And when the two centers of movement (forehand and hindquarters) work together, they create a suspension bridge. This creates a light and springy gait. This is when we describe a horse as "on the aids" and in self-carriage.

It's the primary task of the rider to establish this suspension bridge at every training session. Later, these mechanisms can be further developed into cadence, collection, or extension.

It's important to note that the diaphragm is the musculature that binds these two movement centers together. If the diaphragm is tense, that will lead to problems with breathing and tension in the lumbar region and abdominal muscles. This is what sometimes causes that squeaking noise in stallions and geldings.

➡ **This suspension bridge is especially important for ensuring that pole work leads to positive results!**

➡ **Please don't start working over poles if this basic requirement hasn't been established yet, as doing so could have really negative results for your horse!**

# 3. WALKING EXERCISES WITH POLES

You can recognize a very good walk by the fluidity of movement throughout the horse's body and an even, regular rhythm. Freedom through the shoulders is important; and depending on the tempo, the walk should be ground-covering. The horse should clearly track up with his hindlegs, although to some degree this depends on his conformation. The most common causes for faulty rhythm include incorrect aids from the rider, lack of throughness, and a tight back. In addition, tension or significant one-sidedness on the part of the horse can cause uneven walk strides.

If your veterinarian or trainer can confirm your horse is appropriately sound, riding at the walk over ground poles can be a valuable tool in improving your horse's walk. It's important to eliminate faulty rider aids as a source of problems. To address this, you might practice *Aids at the Walk* (p. 32). Working over ground poles at the walk can help your horse loosen any tension, develop rhythmic and ground-covering strides, and train for various tempos (medium, extended, or collected walk). As the rider, you should aim for a centered seat and suppleness throughout your body—try to disturb your horse as little as possible as he completes the exercises. To help with this, read over *A Centered, Supple Position* (p. 35) and try to apply these concepts to your own riding. Let your reins be as long as possible, so that the horse can walk freely.

## Distance:
About 2.5 feet (.8 meters) for the walk. Shorten for ponies.

## Possible Errors
If the poles are set too far apart, your horse will walk with two feet between the poles.

3. Walking Exercises with Poles

The distance to the first pole is too wide, meaning this horse is going to have difficulty getting to the next pole in the line. Here, it would help to either choose to approach the exercise from a different angle or build in another stride before the first pole.

Eyes up—always! In this picture, you can clearly see how unbalanced the seat becomes when the rider looks down and back. This can cause the horse to hit the last pole with his hind foot, or even get stuck on it!

# SIDE NOTE: AIDS AT THE WALK

This is a little exercise to help you make sure you're using the correct riding aids at the walk (on a straight line).

### The Weight Aids
Because of the horse's pattern of movement at the walk, the rider's hips move in a horizontal figure-eight.

➡ *In order to feel this clearly, you can have a friend or your instructor lead you around for a few minutes at the walk. As they do so, close your eyes. After a few strides, your hips will follow the horse's movement more.*

**Common Errors:**
- Your hips only move from front to back. This can indicate your hips are blocked. I suggest you go and get checked out by a physiotherapist or bodyworker.
- Your hips move asymmetrically. For example, your left hip might move further forward than your right (on a straight line). This can be caused by a physical block in the horse or rider.
- You drive too much with your seat ("pumping"), which can cause the horse's back muscles to lock up.

### The Leg Aids
In accordance with classical technique, instructors will describe alternating leg aids. In order to apply these aids, the rider is always supporting the horse on one side or the other with the leg aids, with the goal of encouraging the horse to walk more fluidly and cover more ground.

It's also acceptable to apply both legs at once. This will often be useful to less experienced riders, who may not be consistently balanced in neutral position yet. When such riders try to apply alternating leg aids, they will often influence the horse in such a way that his walk becomes more like pacing. This is likely due to the rider's own tension. When alternating leg aids are applied correctly, they require a soft contact of the rider's calves against the horse's sides—influencing the horse to move steadily, fluidly, and with ground-covering walk strides.

**Common Errors:**
- You're exerting strong pressure ("gripping") with the calves, which causes the horse to lose throughness.
- You've overused spurs, which makes the horse dull and disturbs his fluidity.

## The Rein Aids

When there are chronic problems with the horse's walk rhythm, he should be ridden long and low, with a long rein. The rider's shoulders, elbows, and wrists must stay loose and only move as much as necessary, always following the movement of the horse's neck.

**Longe-Line Exercise**
- Shake out your wrists for a minute in order to loosen them up.
- Circle your arms to the back.
- Pick up the reins, but not enough to establish a connection with the horse's mouth.
- As soon as your right hip comes forward, move your right forearm forward, and then do the same with the left.

Through this alternating give, you allow the horse's shoulder room to step out. As soon as your seat is correct and supple, you will automatically make this barely visible movement.

**Common Errors:**
- You have "locked" hands—your forearm goes backward when your hip on the same side comes forward, or you are constantly positioning the horse left and right.
- You're positioning the horse too strongly.
- You're forcing the horse's head and neck into position.

In addition, riding on a loose rein will help your horse establish throughness. In general, I recommend keeping your reins as long as possible at the walk. If possible, just walk on the buckle.

When stretching long and low, the horse's nose should not come behind the vertical.

Here, the rider is using a low hand position to encourage the horse to extend the neck. I'd suggest lengthening her stirrups a bit to keep her leg from being bent so much.

# SIDE NOTE: A CENTERED, SUPPLE POSITION

The rider's seat is the basis for every aspect of influence on the horse. All learned aids can only be executed correctly with the foundation of a good seat. Therefore, a centered, supple pelvic position is important—all movements of the limbs depend upon it. So what exactly is a centered position?

A centered position is established through the trunk muscles (abdominals and back). The rider's hips move through relaxation and engagement of these muscle groups. The rider should be able to follow the horse's movement with suppleness, which in turn allows the rider's arms and legs to work independently from her following seat. If the rider is tense or blocked, she will inevitably attempt to remain in balance by pulling her legs up and/or tightening her thighs. Elbows sticking out to the sides are another indicator that the hips aren't supple enough to follow the horse's movement. Other signs of dysfunction might include an upper body that moves like a seesaw or just moves too much altogether, as well as the opposite—almost no movement in the hips at all.

When there's a true line from hip to heel, the rider can achieve a centered, supple following seat.

In addition, there should be a straight line from ear to shoulder to hip, which makes it possible to have a supple following seat.

Here, you can clearly see how the rider's dropped shoulder and the associated collapse through her hip leads to a misalignment of the axes in the horse.

In the photo on the left, the drawn-in line helps you to see how the rider's right shoulder is lower than the left. In the photo on the right, her shoulder position is closer to horizontal. You can clearly see how the degree of the drop in the rider's right shoulder influences the horse's head carriage: in the photo on the left, he's much further from the ideal vertical line than in the photo on the right.

Note that in both photos, the rider's hip has collapsed, causing the horse's hind leg to deviate from the ideal line of travel. When a horse is straight, his hind leg will always follow in the track of his foreleg on the same side.

---

In modern times, many riders spend much of the day sitting at a desk or in a car, which can cause physical blocks as well as deviations in our movement patterns. Therefore, I recommend riders pursue sufficient movement daily and/or select a chair that doesn't allow them to sit still.

➡ **_Along these lines, it's a good idea for a rider to visit a physical therapist or bodyworker who can help loosen physical blocks before they become severe enough to cause faulty movement patterns. You can also use yoga, swimming, and bike riding to improve posture._**

Today, there are many exercise balls and active chairs on the market, which can be used to encourage good posture while seated. A good longe lesson can help, too! Try a variety of options to see what helps.

# 3. Walking Exercises with Poles

## 3.1 The Basic Setup

*To begin with "baby steps," set up 3 poles along the third track, one after the other. This will prevent your horse from leaning on the wall, while at the same time you can use your aids evenly and correctly.*

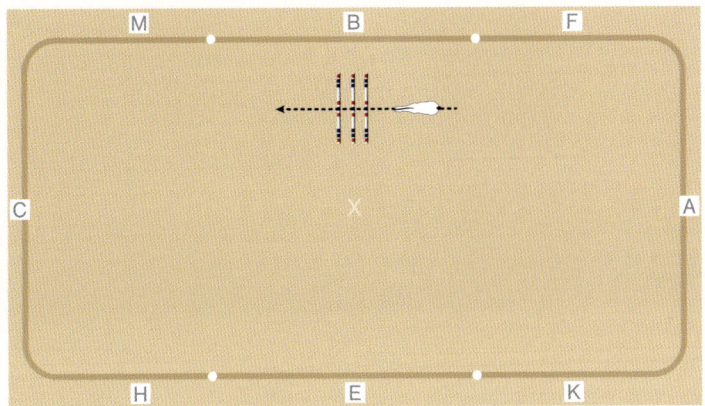

➡ **If you're uncertain, recruit a helper. Ride past the poles. Your helper can watch and let you know whether your horse's footfalls are landing alongside the poles or in between them.**

Ride at the walk on the third track, using the whole arena. Keep an even tempo. It's important to allow your horse to walk without rushing him.

The correct tempo will depend on his conformation and level of training. For a more highly trained horse, you can shorten his frame easily—meaning the horse can better flex the joints of his hindquarters and thereby become more compact. When doing pole work, we don't want to ride the horse slowly; we want to improve his carrying power by building up his muscles. This will in turn lead to a higher and more ground-covering stride. At that point, you can work with a shorter distance between the poles.

As you cross the poles, look ahead and allow your hips to swing with the horse's movement. Guide your horse with a light contact or loose rein.

If the distance between the poles isn't right for your horse, you can ask your helper to increase it or decrease it as needed. As your training continues, it's possible the horse's stride length will change, and you'll need to adjust the distance between the poles accordingly.

## Solutions to Common Problems

**"My horse always bumps the poles and loses his rhythm."**
- Check the distance between the poles. Recruit your helper—she can support you by adjusting the poles as needed.

**"My horse rushes and wants to trot. I always seem to be pulling on the reins."**
- Your horse sounds motivated, and he's making you tense. Take a short break from the poles and instead trot and canter on a circle. This will almost certainly help your horse's concentration.

**Your Horse Has Mastered This Exercise—What's Next?**
➡ After a break, try the next exercise.

# 3.2 Adding More Poles

*You've mastered the basic setup? Then let's move on and add more poles! Instead of using 3 poles, place 6 poles along the diagonal or on the third track, as shown in the arena diagram.*

➡ **Allow your horse to travel with his neck extended over the poles.**

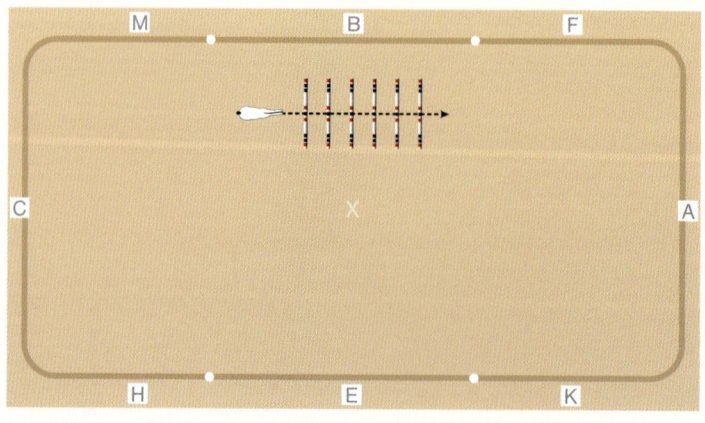

Riding at the walk and using the whole arena, change direction across the long diagonal or travel on the third arena track.

If the distance between poles isn't working, you can have your helper adjust the poles as needed. Again, keep in mind that as you train consistently, the distance needed between the poles may change.

### Solutions to Common Problems

**"My horse gets over the first couple poles without hitting them, but from there on, he has trouble lifting up his feet…"**

- The problem could be a lack of muscle or a lack of motivation. Divide the poles into two sections, so that your horse has a little break in between. As soon as he gets through the first set of poles without hitting them, stop him and praise him extensively. This will both give him a short break and improve his motivation.

If you continue to have problems here, I'd suggest you look to another exercise to try to problem-solve this issue.

**Your Horse Has Mastered This Exercise—What's Next?**
- ➡ You can raise the poles to increase the difficulty.
- ➡ You can train further with one of the following exercises: The Fan at the Walk (3.3); Raise It Up Correctly (3.4).
- ➡ You could also move onto work at the trot with exercises such as The Trio (5.1) or A Line of Six (5.2).

## 3.3 The Fan at the Walk

*Our workout moves on with a fan at the walk. Now it's especially important to keep your eye on the bending line. To prepare, practice the exercises Correct Flexion (2.4) and The Basic Setup (3.1).*

POLE WORK FOR DRESSAGE RIDERS

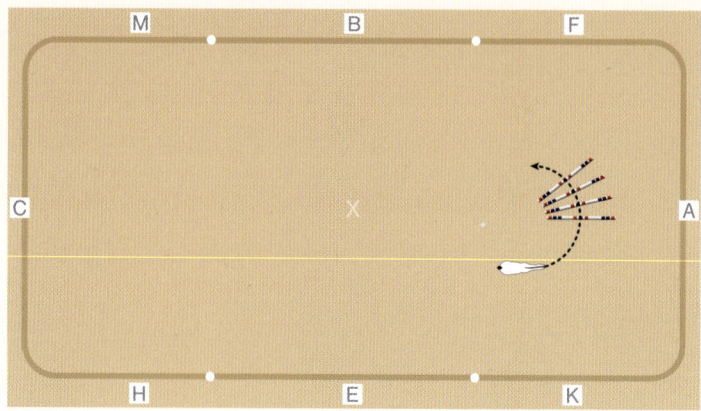

➡ *Toward the center, the distance between the poles will be somewhat smaller. Measure the distance between poles using the middle of the poles for the desired distance.*

At the walk, ride a circle or volte. Keep an even tempo, appropriate for work on a bending line.

For this exercise, you should weight your inside seat bone and send the horse from your inside leg to your outside rein. Your outside leg prevents the horse from going too far sideways. Position the horse with your inside rein, with a light give and take.

And remember: after a break, it's important to change directions and repeat this exercise the other way!

### Solutions to Common Problems

**"My horse steps over two poles at once."**
- Check the distance between the poles. Your helper can assist you to adjust the distances as needed. Or ride toward the outside of the fan instead.

**"My horse falls to the inside."**
- The musculature on the inside of your horse is having difficulty stretching. If he falls out instead when you go the other way, the root cause is likely your horse's natural asymmetry. Apply more inside leg and switch back and forth between this exercise and Lifting the Leg with Correct Flexion (2.4).
- If your horse falls in regardless of the direction, it's likely that he hasn't yet really learned how to bend or he is really tense. In this case, engage your trainer to help find the best solution.

# 3. Walking Exercises with Poles

**Your Horse Has Mastered This Exercise—What's Next?**
- You can also expand the walk fan with additional poles. I'd also suggest you take a break and then train further with the following exercise: Raise It Up Correctly.

## 3.4 Raise It Up Correctly

*Place 3 or more poles along the third track. Raise every other pole up, but just on one side. Alternate which side you're raising.*

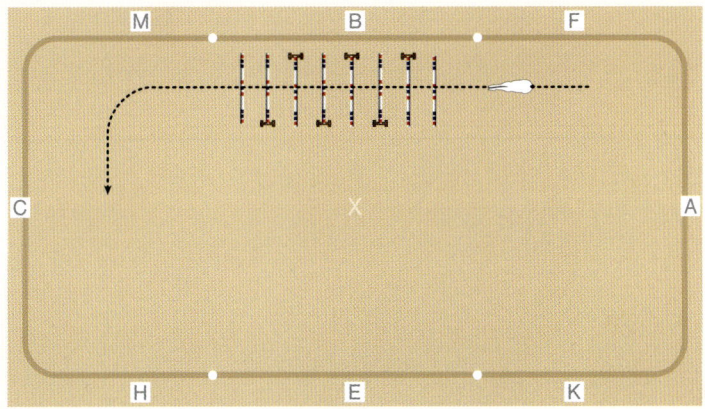

- **Don't raise the first pole or the last pole.**

At the walk, ride the whole arena on the third track. Keep an even tempo. Your horse will need to pick his feet up higher. Look ahead as you ride over the poles and allow your hips to remain relaxed and follow the horse's movement. Guide your horse using only a light rein contact, or with loose reins.

### Solutions to Common Problems

**"My horse always hits the poles and loses his rhythm."**
- Check the distance between poles. Ask your helper to assist you in establishing the correct distances.

POLE WORK FOR DRESSAGE RIDERS

**"My horse rushes and already wants to trot. I find myself constantly pulling back on the reins."**
- Sounds like your horse is motivated and this is causing you to tense up. Take a break from pole work and do some trot or canter work that includes bending lines. Afterwards, your horse should be better able to concentrate on the poles.

**Your Horse Has Mastered This Exercise—What's Next?**
- ➡ I suggest you take a break and then move on with your training using Exercise 3.5. You could also jump to the exercises in chapter 5.
- ➡ If you'd like to get your horse used to trotting over poles without a rider, you can also move onto chapter 4 and work through it parallel to this chapter.

## 3.5 The Raised Fan

*Our walking workout continues with the raised fan. Here, you'll need to pay special attention to the quality of your bending line. To prepare, make sure you've practiced Lifting the Leg with Correct Flexion (2.4) and The Basic Setup (3.1).*

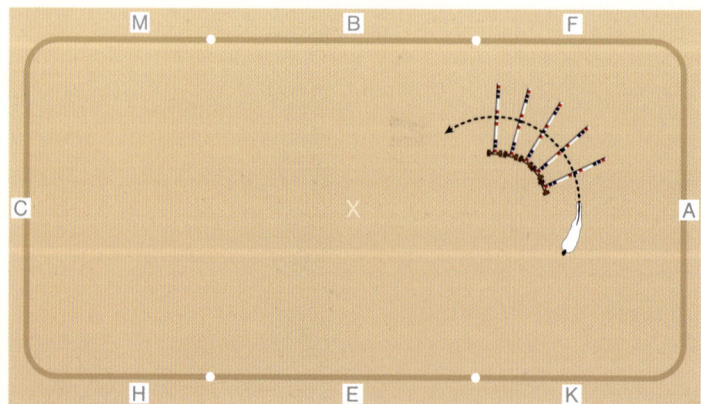

➡ **Toward the middle, the distance between poles will be shorter. Adjust your poles so the distance between them is correct when your horse walks over the middle of the fan.**

# 3. Walking Exercises with Poles

Begin by riding a circle or volte at the walk. Select a tempo that's suitable for a bending line and keep it even.

Remember to apply your bending aids. Weight your inside seat bone, and send the horse from your inside leg to your outside rein. Your outside leg prevents the horse from stepping too far to the outside. Position the horse in the direction of your turn, with a slight give and take on the inside rein.

Make sure to do this exercise in both directions, with a break in between!

## Solutions to Common Problems

### "My horse steps over two poles at once."
- Check the distances and have your helper on the ground make adjustments as needed.
- Or ride this exercise positioned a little further toward the outside of the fan, which automatically makes the distance between poles a bit wider.

### "My horse falls in."
- Your horse is having trouble stretching his inner musculature. Change directions and don't be surprised if he falls out instead in the second direction. If this is the case, his difficulties likely come from his natural asymmetry, which all horses have to some degree. Use your inside leg more strongly to support the bend and go back to Lifting the Leg with Correct Flexion (2.4) for some additional prep work.
- If your horse falls in regardless of the direction of travel, it's likely more of a training problem. He hasn't really understood how to bend correctly or he's too tense. In this case, I think it's best that you work with a trainer to help your horse progress.

### Your Horse Has Mastered This Exercise—What's Next?
⇒ I'd suggest you take a break and then begin with chapter 4 or 6. As soon as your horse gets to the level of training where you're practicing extended and collected walk, you can also work with the exercises in chapter 11—Lengthening the Stride (11.1) and Shortening the Trot on a Bending Line (11.2) in particular.

# 4. TROT WORK ON THE LONGE

# 4. Trot Work on the Longe

There are many benefits to working your horse over poles on the longe line. Without the additional influence of a rider, your horse can loosen up, establish consistent rhythm, and improve the function of his spine thanks to more actively engaged hindquarters.

For young horses, training on the longe line is frequently preferred, but older horses can also benefit from some variety in their daily routine. Longeing can help any horse to build muscle. In addition, the rider can develop a more practiced eye and a better understanding of the horse's biomechanics.

It's a given that the horse must already be established and secure working on the longe line before you attempt longeing over poles. During pole work, the longe line must never touch the ground! In addition, it's crucial that you have suitable materials and positioning for your ground poles, in order to avoid injuries or accidents.

It's important to use ground poles that are in good condition (using broken poles greatly increases the risk of injury to the horse). You can raise the poles

We always hear the truism that the longe line must never touch the ground, but you're probably not any better off hanging it on your horse's ear. The best option of all is for you to hold the longe line in your hand, or ask a helper to assist you if needed.

Use poles that don't splinter, as this reduces the risk of injury to the horse.

There are many options you can use to lift a pole at one end, from cavalletti blocks to baby potties! What's important is that the poles shouldn't be able to roll away easily, while at the same time they shouldn't be fully attached to anything or immobilized.

Experienced riders can estimate the distance between poles by walking it. However, I always recommend beginning with a measuring stick or tape when you set up your poles. I suggest setting up before you bring your horse into the arena.

# 4. Trot Work on the Longe

on blocks made out of plastic or wood. You should not use cavalletti poles with a cross on each end under any circumstances—the X is a hazard, as the longe line can get caught on it easily!

**Distances:**
At the walk—about 2.5 feet (.8 meters)
At the trot—about 4.25 feet (1.3 meters)
At the canter—about 9–10 feet (3 meters)
   For ponies, you will need to shorten it.

The horse must be longed correctly over the poles. If the tempo and approach are not correct, the horse should be asked to turn soon enough to allow him to be longed past the poles instead of over them. Your horse will only benefit from the gymnastic effects of these exercises if his tempo and approach are correct. If you're not sure about this, I suggest you ask an experienced longer or your trainer to help you.

## 4.1 Why Is Trotting Poles Good for Horses?

Trotting over poles develops and confirms a horse's rhythm. For a lot of horses, it's difficult to maintain a steady tempo for a longer period of time, so trot poles can be helpful with this. In addition, trotting over poles improves the horse's coordination and balance. This work also improves the concentration of both the horse and the rider.

The rider develops a feel for the horse's correct trot, with an active hind end and lifted back. She'll also learn to follow her horse's movement, staying loose but with positive tension in her body. The horse's hindquarters are activated, as the horse must lift his hind legs higher in order to make it over the poles. In turn, this develops the interplay of the horse's dorsal (back) and ventral (abdominal)

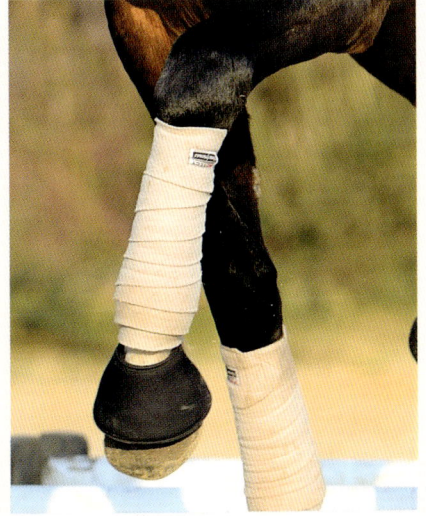

Appropriately selected leg protection is always recommended during pole work.

muscle chains. As the horse's back lifts, his nuchal ligament stretches. In addition, the moment of suspension is improved by this work. As the horse's trot becomes more elastic and powerful, he'll move with more impulsion overall.

Most of the time, when a horse gets too quick at the trot (shorter moment of suspension), it's indicative of either a balance issue or a baseline tempo that is too quick. If he's tense, this can also cause rushed movement. Trot poles can help here, too, by encouraging the horse to maintain a steady tempo and lengthen the moment of suspension.

The source of a lackluster trot can be that the horse has lost his enjoyment in work. To improve the situation, you can offer variety in the horse's training through the use of ground poles, by providing a motivating environment, and by making sure that the rider's aids are correct.

## SIDE NOTE: ARE SIDE-REINS HELPFUL?

When it comes to longeing, the same question always arises: side-reins—yes or no? If yes, what kind?

Side-reins themselves are not the problem, but used incorrectly, they can have disastrous consequences! It always comes down to who's using them, why they're being used, and whether it's the right choice for any individual horse. Therefore, if you're going to use them, it's crucial that you take the time in advance to learn about how they affect the horse and the many types of side-reins available.

Generally speaking, longeing with side-reins is recommended. You can also find a variety of longeing systems that can be used to help frame the horse from behind. Please avoid the use of any auxiliary reins that force the horse into too deep of a frame; in addition to the usual reasons for avoiding this, there's also a danger with pole work that the horse's front legs will get caught.

If your horse has a tendency to throw his head in the air, you should have his movement evaluated by an expert. As described in the section *Positive Tension* (p. 27), your horse might be experiencing a blockage or tension in his forehand.

Side-reins should always help the horse find the correct frame, which in turn will allow him to move most correctly. If that's not happening, either the side-reins are attached incorrectly or you haven't selected the right type of auxiliary rein for this point in the horse's training. If you're not sure what to use, you can't go wrong with a cavesson without side-reins!

4. Trot Work on the Longe

## 4.2 Finding the Way

*Begin with 4 poles, placed in pairs on a circle. In this exercise, we aren't starting the real work yet. It's much more important for the horse to get used to the poles, and for the person longeing to find the best place to stand and the best way to guide the horse. Experienced longers can skip this exercise.*

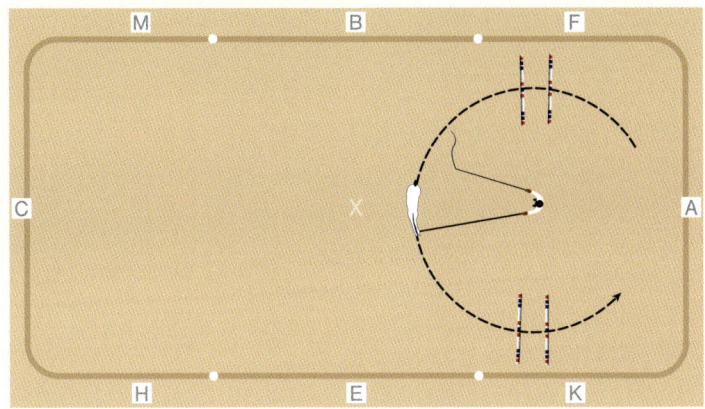

First, longe the horse around the poles.

The horse is really close to the pole. Since his hind end is really active, this might cause him to step on the pole.

➡ **Stand in one spot so your horse can move in an even circle around you at the trot.**

Longe your horse around you, first at the walk and then at the trot. Make sure your horse crosses over the centers of the poles and therefore won't need to change his rhythm as he moves around the circle. If you see his rhythm change, the distance between the poles might be incorrect, or the horse might not be achieving the correct distance. Try making the size of your circle bigger or smaller. As you do this, don't walk yourself out farther; lengthen or shorten your longe line as necessary instead.

➡ **Don't arrange the poles in a "fan"—place them parallel to one another.**

## Solutions to Common Problems

**"My horse wants to shorten up and falls to the inside."**
- Use the whip to frame your horse. By pointing it toward his shoulder, help the horse understand that he must maintain the circle.

4. Trot Work on the Longe

> **"My horse pulls to the outside and doesn't want to trot over the poles…"**
> - It sounds as if it's not clear to your horse that you're choosing the direction, or his motivation for pole work leaves something to be desired. Find a competent trainer to help you practice.

**Your Horse Has Mastered This Exercise—What's Next?**
➡ I suggest you move onto the next exercise.

## 4.3 Finding Rhythm

*Now, we want to establish the correct rhythm before we begin the actual work. Place 4 poles one after the next on a circle, with the correct distance between them.*

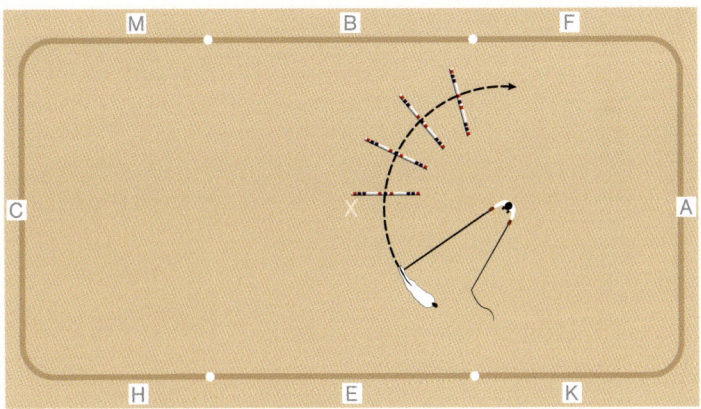

➡ ***Always measure the distance between poles at the middle of the poles.***

Longe your horse over the poles repeatedly, until he finds a good rhythm and will trot over the poles with relaxation. You can also set up 4 more poles on the opposite side of the circle, which will increase the effects of the training. Repeat this exercise a few times in a row before you move on to the next exercise.

The horse is finding his way over the poles, but his side-reins are too tight for him to stretch correctly at the trot.

For the moment, don't try to advance. Practice this exercise a few times first, until your horse really has it down!

## Solutions to Common Problems

### "My horse loses his rhythm over the poles."
- This could have to do with the distance between the poles. See if you can solve this problem by making your circle bigger or smaller, which will position the horse to trot over a different place along the lengths of the poles.

### "As my horse trots over the poles, he always brings his head up and extends his lower neck."
- In this case, your horse is trying to lift his forehand over the poles with the help of his neck. Instead, he should lift his chest and not need to use his lower neck muscles. You might find a massage helps him. Talk to your horse's physical therapist or bodyworker. Side-reins will not help here; adding them would only mean the horse must push his lower neck muscles against the side-reins, too. If it's a very mild problem, though, side-reins can

help him stabilize himself. Talk it over with your trainer. Typically, after some repetitions, the horse will figure it out for himself and realize that using his lower neck muscles doesn't help him. Then he'll stretch his nuchal ligament, lift his chest with the help of the poles, and arrive in the desired forward and downward stretch.

**"My horse constantly trips over the poles or doesn't lift his legs up high enough."**
- Your horse has a passive forehand, and it isn't lifting. He needs to learn to lift his chest. Physical therapists have good massage techniques that can help with this. You can also work wonders by riding him over raised poles, as well as up and down hills. These strategies develop his hindquarters, which will have a positive effect on the forehand. Speak with an expert to develop a training plan for daily work.

**"My horse can't get over the poles with his hind legs."**
- This could be due to tension in his loin area, just behind the saddle, or a blocked lumbosacral joint. Expert advice is warranted here.
    If tension or blocks are not discovered, you might explore working with a resistance band or longeing system that helps engage the hindquarters. This can help encourage the horse to bring his hind legs further underneath himself, which will tilt his pelvis and help relieve any tension.

**Your Horse Has Mastered This Exercise—What's Next?**
➡ Wonderful! You can now move onto a light workout.

## 4.4 A Light Workout

*Let's get started with a trot workout on the longe line. Place 4 poles on a circle at the correct distance from one another. On the opposite side of the circle, place 4 more with both sides raised—see diagram below.*

➡ ***If the distance between the 4 poles doesn't work out, you can adjust the distances or direct the horse toward the outer edge of the poles (a bigger circle).***

# POLE WORK FOR DRESSAGE RIDERS

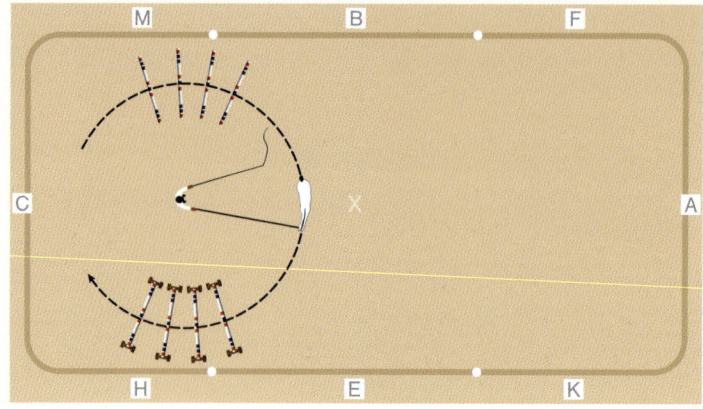

Longe your horse over the poles until he finds a good rhythm and demonstrates relaxation while trotting over the poles. The horse should maintain the same rhythm before, over, and after the poles. He should also learn not to hit or catch on the raised poles. Repeat this exercise a few times back-to-back before changing to another exercise.

Begin this exercise by longeing your horse around the outside of the poles first, allowing him to establish the correct tempo before asking him to trot over the poles.

# 4. Trot Work on the Longe

## Solutions to Common Problems

- Take a look back at the suggestions for common problems and relevant solutions throughout this chapter.

**Your Horse Has Mastered This Exercise—What's Next?**
➡ Fantastic. Now the workout can begin with 4.5: Abs, Legs, and Butt for Your Horse." Let's do this!

## 4.5 Abs, Legs, and Butt for Your Horse

*Now we're digging deeper, and the real workout is about to begin. Place 8 poles on the circle. Raise every other pole on the outside, and the others on the inside. Arrange your circle along the third track off the arena rail.*

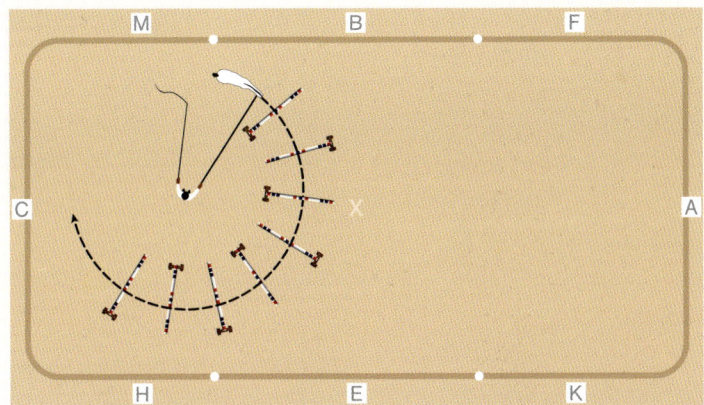

➡ **When your horse's inside hind trots over the pole ahead of the outside hind, it will be easier for him to trot over the poles with correct bend and without hitting them.**

Remember to first longe your horse around the outside of the poles at the trot, and then make your circle smaller until he's trotting over the middle of the poles. In this exercise, it's really important to get the horse over the middle of the poles, and most horses will seek the middle for themselves, since both the outsides and insides of the poles are raised in different places.

> **Solutions to Common Problems**
>
> - You notice that your horse always performs differently depending on his direction of travel? Check out the section about asymmetry beginning on this page.

**Your Horse Has Mastered This Exercise—What's Next?**
- ➡ You can repeat this exercise for a longer period each time, until you're ready to move on to the next exercise.
- ➡ You can move on to Exercise 4.6 (p. 63).
- ➡ How about a workout for you? Saddle up your horse and try Exercise 6.4 (p. 90). You're already familiar with the setup.

# SIDE NOTE: NATURALLY CROOKED OR NICE AND STRAIGHT?

A pole workout is, of course, not the only solution for a crooked horse. Pole work does help the horse fix his natural asymmetry, since his movement centers are required to work together. However, a horse that is truly ridden correctly won't need pole work to become straight. And at the same time, pole work executed incorrectly can cause a natural asymmetry to get worse—with consequences.

**In other words: Pole workouts can help a horse become straighter—as long as they are executed correctly.**

When a horse drifts to the inside or outside on a circle, you might say that he's "falling onto his shoulder." That is true—however, you should be aware that a horse can only "fall onto his shoulder" when his movement centers (forehand and hindquarters) are not working correctly. They are either too passive or too tense. The origin of the problem will be found in instability in the outer musculature (shoulder and pelvic girdle).

Therefore, to correct a horse's natural asymmetry, the top priority should be to stabilize the shoulder girdle with support from the hindquarters. In order for a horse to travel straight and be able to bend correctly in both directions, he must actively be able to resist the centrifugal force of his chest and pelvis through the turn. To achieve this, he must track up with his hind legs. The rider can use her outside rein to help the horse achieve stability.

**So how exactly does pole work help the horse?**
Pole work alone won't help, as explained above, but can support the horse by encouraging his hindquarters to become more active. In addition, it can help correct a horse whose natural stance is too narrow or too wide. Pole work helps to build muscles in the hindquarters. It also helps the forehand to engage with positive tension and lift the chest. But all this is no substitute for good, correct riding.

**How can we support a horse's straightness during pole work?**
We are aiming to strengthen the shoulder girdle and avoid a twisting of the chest, to ensure that the horse's footfalls and legs are on the correct axes. You can find more information about correct bend on page 16.

Asymmetry in the horse, whether it's naturally occurring or has developed during training, is a big topic. That could be a book in and of itself. I'll try to keep it short and simple here: when we talk about a horse with naturally occurring asymmetry, we refer to a hollow side and a stiff side.

On the hollow side, the lateral muscles are shortened. In this direction, the horse can bend more easily, but is difficult to correct with the inside aids. When it comes to longeing exercises, attempting to address this side directly is impractical, as we don't have outside aids to use (except for double longeing). In this direction, the horse wants to drift to the outside.

On the stiff side, the horse's muscles are longer and are more difficult to shorten. Here, it's useful to correct the horse with the inside aids, but he'll be more difficult to bend in this direction. In addition, the horse will want to fall to the inside and make his circle smaller in the stiffer direction.

I don't find it accurate to speak about a "good" or "bad" side. Both directions have their positive and negative attributes. We want to help our horses improve in both directions of travel, and I'll describe how to do so using the following exercises.

## A) Pole Workouts for Horses Who Fall In

*Does your horse always want to fall in and make a smaller circle on the longe line? Or, when ridden, does the horse barge through his inside shoulder?*

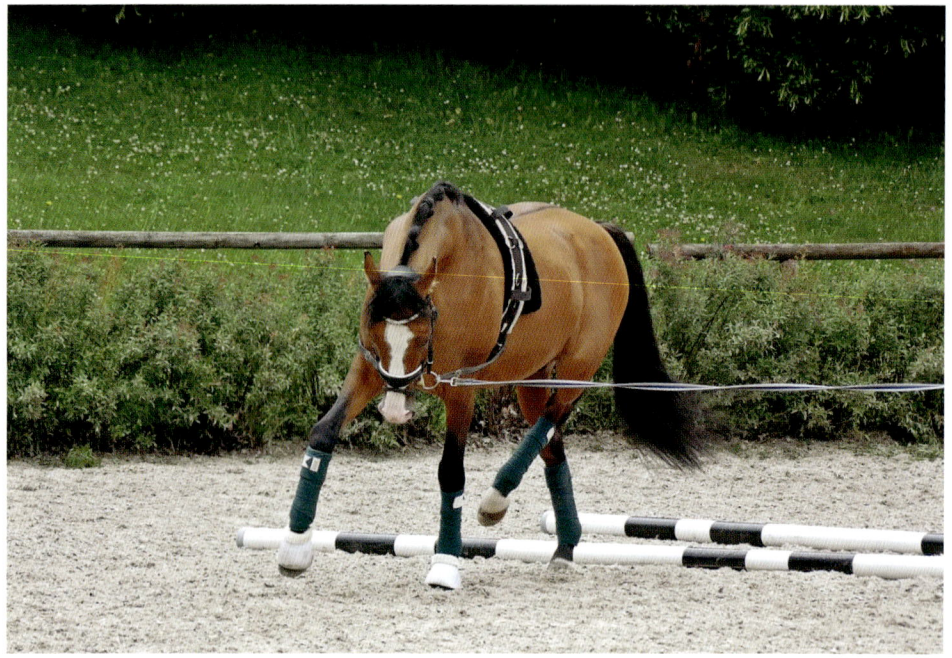

The horse is obviously pulling to the outside; his axes have become misaligned, and he can no longer trot with good impulsion.

---

Here, you can see the horse remains unbalanced. Without a rider's (or longer's) aids, the horse finds it difficult to bend. His shoulder girdle and pelvic girdle will benefit from further training.

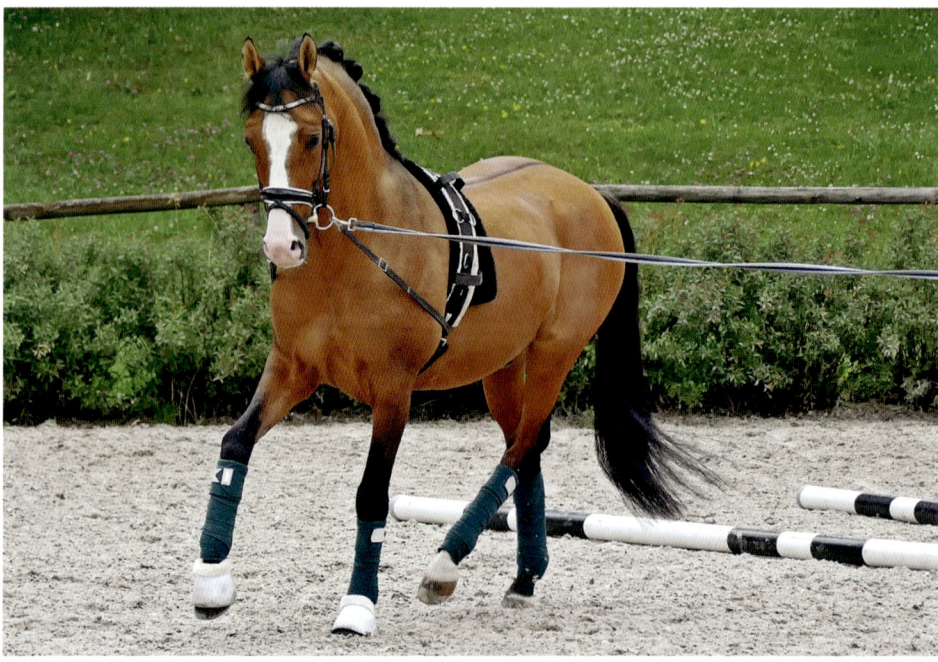

4. Trot Work on the Longe

The horse is falling heavily onto his inside shoulder and looking to the outside.

Distracted by external stimuli, this horse is no longer concentrating on the poles. Here, it would be wise to refocus his attention. Most of the time, voice aids can be really useful here. Raising the poles won't help, as in this case it's not an issue of asymmetry.

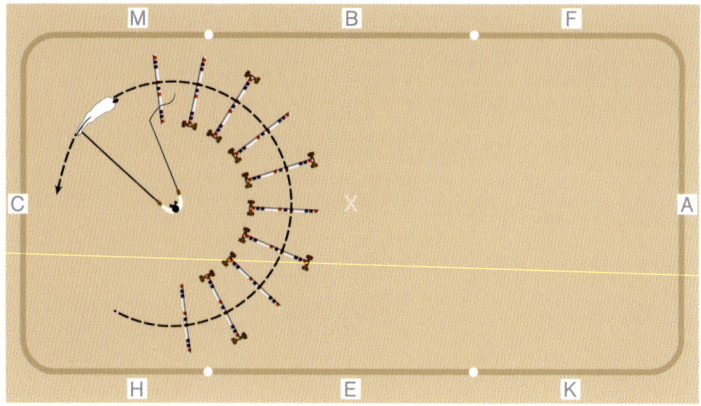

Here's an arena setup that not only encourages your horse to lift his forehand, but will also strengthen the inside of his shoulder girdle. Place 6 to 10 poles on a circle. Raise every other pole on the inside of the circle. For the alternating poles, raise up both sides. Don't raise up the first and last poles at all—they should lie flat.

➡ *If your horse needs to improve his strength and lift on the inside, you can raise the poles on the inside.*

Longe your horse over the middle of the poles. He'll find it very difficult to fall to the inside, as the inside of the poles is higher than the outside.

---

The poles raised on the inside are helping this pony lift his inside shoulder. His muscle chains are working really well together here, although I'd like to see his face a bit more ahead of the vertical. For that reason, I'd loosen the side-reins slightly. (See more on this horse on page 68).

# 4. Trot Work on the Longe

## Solutions to Common Problems

**"My horse no longer falls to the inside, but drifts to the outside instead."**
- It could be that your horse is seeking an easy way out and therefore is now drifting to the outside. If this happens, you should alternate between raising the poles at the inside end and raising them at the outside end, creating a cross that will encourage the horse to see the "middle of the road" as the optimal and easiest line of travel.

**"After just a couple of rounds, my horse is tired out."**
- It makes perfect sense that your horse might be wiped out after a round or two of this exercise, which demands a lot from one side of his body. Make sure you're building sufficient break time into your training. Note that your horse has adopted compensatory postures, probably originating with his natural asymmetry, and as a result he has much weaker muscles on one side of his body; he's going to need time to build or re-build those muscles. With the help of a trainer or a friend with a good eye, you need to pay close attention to your horse's overall axial alignment. Especially over the poles, the axes need to be aligned.

## B) Pole Workouts for Horses Who Fall Out

*Does your horse always fall out on the longe line and struggle to stay on the line of travel? Or, when ridden, does your horse push through the outside shoulder?*

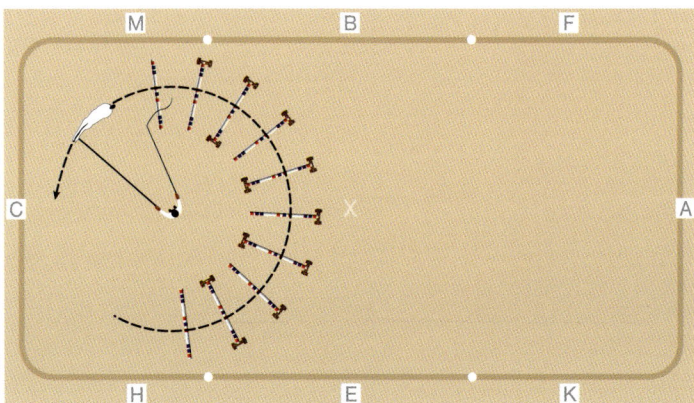

Poles lifted on the outside help this pony lift his outside shoulder.

Now let's get started with a pole workout that will strengthen the outside of your horse's shoulder girdle and lift the forehand. Place 6–10 poles on a circle. Raise every other pole on the outside, and then raise the remaining poles on both sides. Don't raise the first pole or the last—these should lie flat.

➡ *If your horse needs to improve strength and lift on the outside, you can raise the poles on the outside.*

Longe your horse over the middle of the poles. Your horse will find it much harder to fall out, as the outside of the poles is higher than the inside.

## Solutions to Common Problems

**"My horse no longer drifts to the outside; he's falling in instead."**
- It's normal for horses to look for the easiest way out. If this happens, you can resolve it by alternating between raising the poles at the inside end and raising them at the outside end, creating a cross that will encourage the horse to see the "middle of the road" as the optimal and easiest line of travel.

4. Trot Work on the Longe

**"My horse loses his strength after a round or two."**
- It makes perfect sense that your horse might be wiped out after a round or two of this exercise, which demands a lot from one side of his body. Make sure you're building sufficient break time into your training. Note that your horse has adopted compensatory postures, probably originating with his natural asymmetry, and as a result he has much weaker muscles on one side of his body; he's going to need time to build or re-build those muscles. With the help of a trainer or a friend with a good eye, you need to pay close attention to your horse's overall axial alignment. Especially over the poles, the axes need to be aligned.

## 4.6 The Endless Circle

*This exercise not only develops muscular strength, it's also good for conditioning and coordination. Place poles all along the circle, using the second or third arena track. You can also raise some of the poles to increase the difficulty of the exercise. Near X, leave half a dozen feet (a couple of meters) free, to allow you to guide the horse onto or out of the circle at any time.*

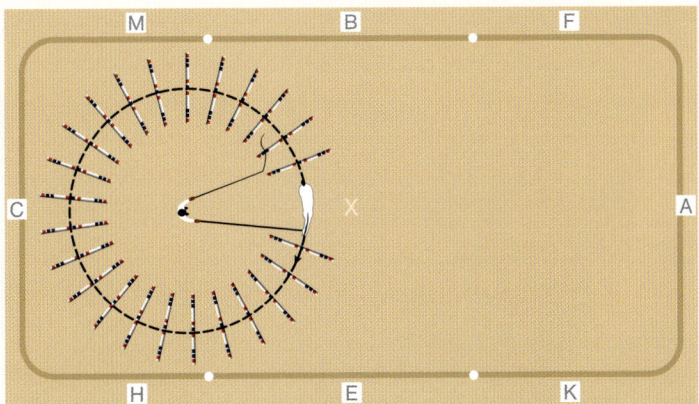

➡ **Place the outer edge of the poles approximately 9.5 feet (3 meters) apart on the circle, and the inner edge of the poles 4.25 feet (1.3 meters), which will allow you to execute this exercise at the trot and the canter.**

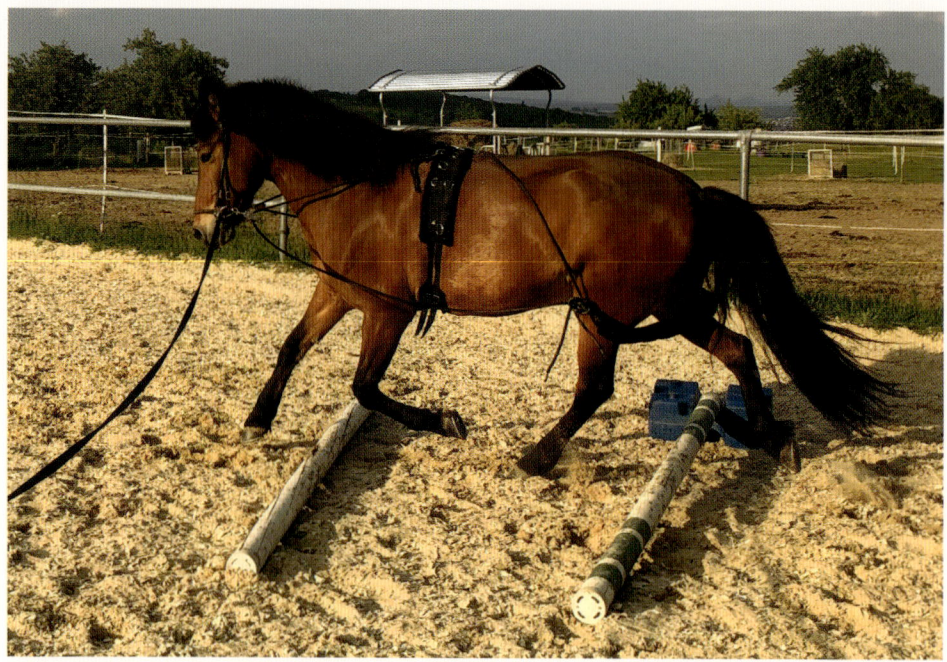

You can guide the horse to enter or exit the circle at various points. Here, we're using a gap on the open side of the circle.

This exercise is difficult, but effective. I've included variations of this exercise throughout the book, and you'll find them highly effective at improving the horse's muscular strength.

Because this exercise is so demanding, you should ease into it after several weeks of pole workouts. Gradually increase the number of poles, and avoid overwhelming your horse!

Longe your horse at the trot either inside or outside of the poles, allowing him to find an even tempo. Next, make your circle bigger or smaller, whichever is necessary to position the horse so he's trotting over the middle of the poles. Praise your horse during this exercise and support him with your voice and whip aids.

Remember to always build in breaks and changes of direction. This exercise can be repeated weekly. Just be careful that you don't overface your horse. He needs to slowly acclimate to this exercise and to any raising of the poles.

If you've set the poles up 9–10 feet (3 meters) apart on the outer edge of the poles, as described, you can also ask the horse to go from a trot to a canter over the poles. Many horses find the canter easier, so make sure your horse doesn't start always picking up the canter of his own accord.

## 4. Trot Work on the Longe

It's always the goal for the movement developed over the poles to continue afterwards.

For this five-year-old, we've eliminated every other pole. This reduces the level of difficulty for now.

If at any point your horse starts to stumble or no longer is lifting his feet correctly, you should gently encourage him with your whip. Then, as soon as he comes to the gap in the poles by X, adjust the size of your circle so he's traveling to the inside or outside of the poles. At that point, transition down to a walk and allow him to enjoy a break.

### Solutions to Common Problems

- There are many challenges associated with this exercise. You'll find most problems repeat themselves, so it's a good idea to go back and read the other solutions to common problems presented in this chapter—you'll likely find an answer that works for you there.

**Your Horse Has Mastered This Exercise—What's Next?**
➡ This is one of the most difficult exercises in this book! Have you already tried raising some of the poles? This will increase the difficulty. Otherwise, I'd say: saddle up your horse and continue with the exercises in chapters 5 and 6.

# EXTRA: ABS, LEGS, AND BUTT FOR RIDERS

As you've undoubtedly noticed already, preparing the arena for the horse's workout over poles is also a good workout for the rider or longer. All of those poles and blocks must be carried into the arena, set up, and then taken down and put away again.

If you can arrange to train with a group, it means a little less work for each person to do. Likewise, a tractor with a trailer cart can save you a lot of steps.

However, you can also use this setup time as an opportunity for conditioning. Many people drag themselves to the gym hoping for tight abs, muscular legs, and a strong rear. For you, this now comes included with your riding and pole workout! Isn't that great? And yes, you must use the correct technique—just like your horse—if you want to stay sound.

Be kind to your back when you lift poles.

When you lift weight using your back alone, you task the last intervertebral disc of your spine with lifting up to 12 times the actual weight you're trying to move, thanks to torque and leverage. Therefore, it's important to lift with the right technique!

- Step up close to the pole, block, or whatever object you're going to lift. The closer you stand to the object, the easier it will be on your back when you lift it.
- Bend your legs or squat; this will let you use your leg muscles to lift the weight.
- With a straight back, fold your upper body forwards a little and grip the pole with both hands. As you do so, engage your abdominal and back muscles, which will stabilize your trunk. Avoid hollowing or rounding your back.
- Lift the pole evenly, from the middle, with control. Straighten through your legs and torso.
- As you're carrying the pole, you should avoid rotating your spine. If you need to turn, do so with your whole body, not your torso alone.

Lifting with good technique leads to an even distribution of weight along the intervertebral discs. This protects the spine from being overused in any one place, and from degenerative injury. This is easier to accomplish with end blocks if you carry them two at a time.

As long as you've got the right lifting technique, you'll be strengthening your legs, glutes, and abdominal muscles through all the repetitive lifting involved with setting up your arena. By carrying poles, you'll strengthen your arms and chest muscles, which contribute to upright posture. You'll see—we humans really aren't that different from our horses! We also need to maintain a lifted chest and tucked pelvis in order to achieve healthy movement patterns.

If you wish to enhance your training, you can even add a few exercises without lifting poles. For example, cross one leg over the other as you step sideways. In order to ensure correct "flexion" of your joints, make sure you lift your legs up high as you do this, which will allow your hips to fall to one side or the other; just as for horses, this relaxes and strengthens the muscles of the lumbar area. Think about how you would want your horse to move in order to strengthen his back. This exercise also supports the development of a supple seat in the saddle. It's worth it.

Finally, although they are lighter, I suggest you avoid using plastic poles. They're so light that if the horse hits them, they will roll too easily, and they can also fall off a block easily when lifted. This doesn't mean you have to go back to those heavy wooden cavalletti that were so popular back in the day. There are lots of great options now for medium-weight poles and blocks to use for your pole workout.

## A Short Case Study

For the purposes of our case study, we'll refer to our subject as "Pony." Pony has a prior condition. Two years ago, Pony suffered a right hind tendon injury, which has since healed. Because of the compensatory movement habits he settled into while it was healing, Pony developed an asymmetry, and his back musculature has built unevenly. Pony has a hard time bending right and constantly leans on his right shoulder. Given this, we can determine that Pony's left side is the hollow side, and his right side is the stiff side. In addition, his hindquarters remain passive, and the hind legs are too close together when standing. Pony is using the muscles along the underside of his neck to lift his forehand, which means his chest is not engaged positively and instead is tight. Thanks to his poorly muscled hindquarters and tense forehand, Pony cannot properly develop through his back.

However, regular osteopathic treatments throughout his two-year recovery eliminated physiological blocks that might otherwise have developed.

Pony's training plan includes regular arena and trail riding, as well as workouts over poles. In this case, we utilized the exercises found in the section *Naturally Crooked or Nice and Straight?* (p. 56) Specifically, I recommended Exercise A for Pony while tracking right, and Exercise B while tracking left. To allow his back to improve and his movement patterns to change, we chose to do these pole workouts on the longe line. We selected a longeing system for our auxiliary reins. This helped Pony by framing his hindquarters and encouraging him to step up actively behind. In addition, the longeing system framed Pony laterally and supported him in finding the correct working frame.

After just three training sessions, we could already see the first signs of success. Pony's hindquarters were much more active, and his exterior muscles were building up. Likewise, the muscles along the underside of Pony's neck were less noticeable and his bend to the right was much better.

As Pony is blessed with a strong pony brain, he learns really quickly but also knows how to avoid work. Therefore, we gradually added more and more poles to the training sessions. Soon, we were using Exercise 4.5 (p. 55) in combination with Exercises A and B. After many weeks of training, the signs of success developed into a major victory. Pony now has enough strength to master new, fully sound movement patterns, and to excel at the pole workouts. His movement has improved dramatically, and his hindquarters are noticeably stronger and more active. In turn, his back muscles have improved. Pony will continue pole workouts to further his development.

## 4. Trot Work on the Longe

Because Pony doesn't want to bend right and instead falls onto his right shoulder, we've lifted the inside ends of the poles.

In this picture, you can clearly see how impulsion is traveling through the whole body and all the muscle chains are working together.

To prevent Pony from falling out and help lift his outside shoulder, we've lifted the outside ends of the poles here.

# 5. TROT POLES ON STRAIGHT LINES

For the rider, it's relatively easy to trot the horse over poles on a straight line; however, it does require a certain amount of effort for the horse, who needs to correctly engage and relax all of his muscles over a longer period of time. As he's trotting over poles, all his muscle chains must work together. For example, if the horse's shoulder girdle is weak on one side, he'll immediately begin falling out over that shoulder as soon as he starts to fatigue. When this occurs, he'll no longer travel over the middle of the poles, or he'll start hitting the poles, or both.

When this occurs, it shows you clearly which muscles your horse needs to train better. When you encounter difficulties, you can simply go back to an exercise on a bending line or continue training with the exercises in the section *Naturally Crooked or Nice and Straight?* (p. 56). It's always fine to backtrack until your horse has built up the necessary strength to progress further.

If you find your horse constantly catches a hind leg on the poles, that means his hindquarters need to be more active. His frontal thigh muscles need to be built up. Give your horse some support by framing him with your legs. Whether you're riding on the flat or over poles, it's important for the horse's pelvis to tuck correctly.

If the horse has problems with his iliosacral joint, and subsequently with tucking his pelvis, I'd suggest you take a look at his hooves. If the soles of the hoof are visible longer than usual when you watch him from behind, this confirms that the pelvis is not tucking correctly.

In addition, you can improve your horse's rhythm, ability to cover ground, cadence, and activity depending on how much distance you put between the poles. However, it's important that you position them relatively close together at first, allowing your horse to develop the necessary strength and endurance before you move them farther apart.

## SIDE NOTE: THE AIDS AT THE TROT

The trot is a two-beat gait with four phases. This means there's a diagonal pair of legs touching the ground (in the "standing leg phase"), and at the same time, there's an opposing diagonal pair of legs in the air (the "hanging leg phase"). In between, there's a moment of suspension, where all four legs are off the ground. The goal is springy steps, executed playfully and lightly with the power of the horse's muscles. This protects the horse's joints and soft tissues. Therefore, it's crucial for the horse's centers of movement to turn correctly and for

In these photos, you can see the difference between posting and sitting trot. At posting trot, the upper body is angled slightly forward, which supports the horse's forward movement. While posting the trot, remember to allow your heel to come down by opening your knee a bit when you post. It's easy to see the difference between a tight and relaxed knee in these photos.

the horse to be ridden with positive tension. The rider also needs to maintain positive tension in her body. To this end, the rider's ability to maintain a central position and follow the horse's movement is an essential goal.

Through a correct and supple following of the horse's movement while maintaining a central position, the rider helps the horse alternately engage and relax his back and maintain his rhythm. As you begin the following exercises, ride at a posting trot, to encourage your horse to swing over the poles more energetically. For most riders, this would at first be very difficult to achieve at sitting trot. To prepare, review *Posting Trot Correctly* (p. 104).

Always ride over the middle of the poles. As you do so, make sure your horse maintains the same rhythm before, over, and after the poles. Frame the horse with your legs, encouraging him to trot straight over the poles. As he's doing this, avoid blocking him or holding too tight with your reins. Don't use your reins as a brake—instead, drive your horse from your legs toward the bit. This will allow his chest to lift and his hind legs to step up actively under his center of gravity. The desired result is a lowering of his pelvis. For more details about this and why it's important, review *Half-Halts and Full Halts* (p. 107).

➡ **Use poles that are about 11.5 feet (3.5 meters) long, ideally with a circumference of about 3–4 inches (8–10 cm).**

A friendly reminder: Take a break and then make sure to complete the exercise in the other direction.

## Distance:
At the trot—approximately 4.25 feet (1.3 meters)
Shorten the distance for ponies

# 5.1 The Trio

*To introduce this exercise with "baby steps," start with 3 poles in a line on the third track of the arena. By positioning them off the rail, you prevent the horse from developing the habit of "leaning" on the rail for support. You can use your aids instead to frame him correctly and in good balance.*

➡ **Look up and over the poles. If you're uncertain, find a ground person to assist you. First ride wide, past the poles. Your helper should tell you whether the horse's footfalls would have naturally landed in between the poles, if he had been moving over them instead of beside them.**

POLE WORK FOR DRESSAGE RIDERS

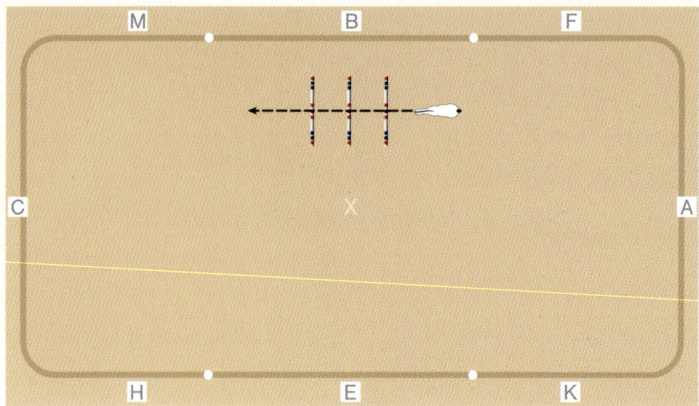

Ride at the trot on the third track, using the whole arena. Keep an even tempo. The correct tempo will depend on your horse's conformation and level of training. With a more highly trained horse, you'll be able to shorten his frame easily, meaning the horse can better flex the joints of his hindquarters and thereby become more compact.

When doing pole work, we don't want to ride the horse slowly; we want to improve his carrying power by building up his muscles. This will in turn lead to a higher and more ground-covering stride. At that point, you can choose to work with a shorter distance between the poles.

Look at the distances between the poles and loosely follow the horse's movement with your hips.

## Solutions to Common Problems

**"My horse keeps hitting the poles and losing his rhythm."**
- Check the distances between poles. An assistant on the ground can support you with adjusting the poles.

**"My horse gets quicker and quicker..."**
- Go back to Exercise 2.2 (p. 20).

You can also combine the two exercises. Traveling on the third track, cross over the poles. Your horse will get quicker. After the poles, turn toward the rail and ride a half circle to change direction. As soon as possible, return to the third track. Stay at the trot in the new direction. When your horse gets quick again, whether the poles are there or not, repeat the half circle. Over time, your horse will learn to maintain his rhythm.

## 5. Trot Poles on Straight Lines

Think and look forward as you cross the poles. Your elastic seat will support your horse in maintaining an even tempo.

**Your Horse Has Mastered This Exercise—What's Next?**
- I suggest you take a short break and then move on to the next exercise in this chapter.

## 5.2 A Line of Six

*Let's get to the next step in your workout. Place 6 poles in a line, as in the previous exercise. Please make sure you only add poles once your horse can complete the previous exercise (3 poles)—without hitting his feet. This might happen in one training session, but it may also take several days. Don't overwhelm your horse by using too many poles too soon!*

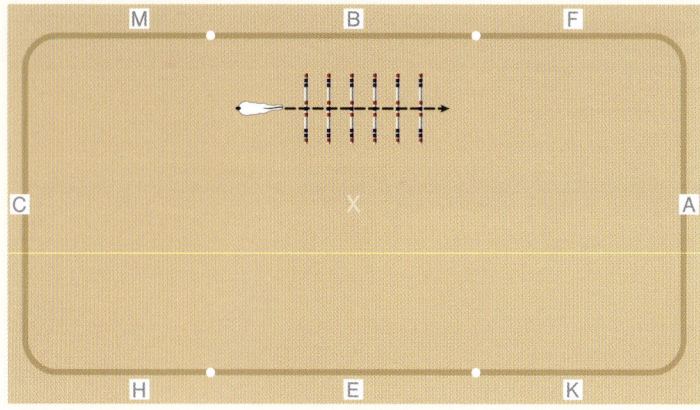

➡ *Imagine that there's one more pole to ride over at the end of the line. This will help you and your horse maintain the engagement needed for the horse to clear the last pole without hitting a hind foot.*

Ride this exercise just like the last one. If you want to increase the degree of difficulty, you can raise the poles or work with low cavalletti. Always make sure your horse continues to use his movement centers correctly and is being ridden with positive tension. Prepare your horse with half-halts. Review *Half-Halts and Full Halts* (p. 107).

When trotting over poles, it can be very helpful for the rider to sit the trot, so long as her hips remain following and elastic. Smile as you ride this exercise; it'll relax your muscles and help you remain elastic and centered.

# 5. Trot Poles on Straight Lines

## Solutions to Common Problems

**"My horse can do 3 poles without a problem, but with 6 he always hits one."**
- Your horse has far too little muscle and needs to build up his strength. Split the six poles into two groups of three. This way, your horse has time in between to regroup.

**Your Horse Has Mastered This Exercise—What's Next?**
➡ Take a break and then move on to the next exercise.

## 5.3 The Long Line

*As the next step, place up to 16 poles, one after another, along the third track. Above all, this exercise requires correct collaboration between the horse's dorsal and ventral muscle chains.*

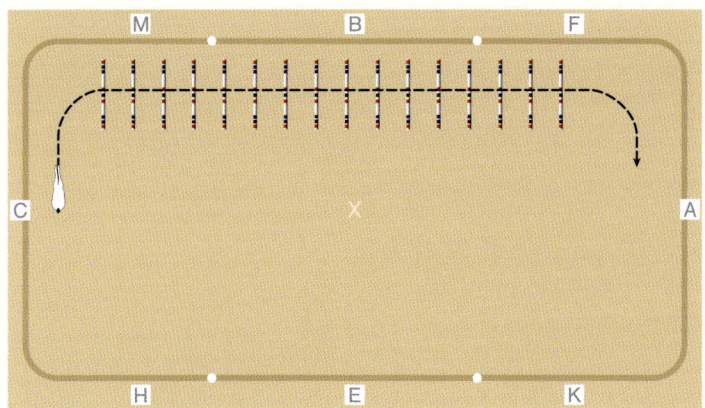

➡ *Don't let the number of poles bother you. If this exercise is difficult, divide the poles into two groups of eight, or leave additional space between two poles.*

It's a challenge for horse and rider to maintain positive tension for such a long time. Be sure you're breathing, and stay elastic in your ankles, in order to avoid tensing up.

Start with just a few additional poles and then build from there, making sure your horse is able to trot confidently over the poles without hitting any. This might happen in one training session or it might take many tries. Please don't overface your horse with too many poles! Make sure your horse is moving correctly. If you're not sure, ask a trainer or experienced rider to help you.

### Solutions to Common Problems

#### "My horse just gets quicker over the poles."
- Your horse does not have enough strength. You can work with fewer poles for now, increasing the number over time.

#### "My horse no longer wants to go over poles…"
- Have you overtaxed your horse? Or was there an upset the last time you went over the poles? For example, if your horse hit a pole during a previous attempt and is now traveling unevenly, you should take a break from your training and seek expert advice. If he's not having a physical problem, it might be that he needs more motivation for this challenging exercise. Praise your horse extensively and exuberantly after every successful attempt.

5. Trot Poles on Straight Lines

- Build in more breaks, so that your horse has a chance to recover from the challenging work. Otherwise, he'll develop muscle soreness, which can be very uncomfortable.

**Your Horse Has Mastered This Exercise—What's Next?**
➡ After a break, I'd suggest you train further with the next exercise.

## 5.4 The Long Line with Angled Poles

*Here's the next step for your workout. Place 16 poles, one after another, along the third track. Some of them can be placed at an angle, as shown in the diagram. Now you'll be asking your horse for concentration and coordination.*

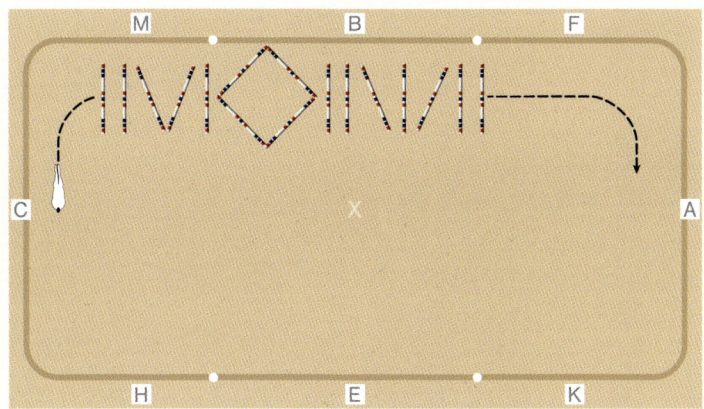

➡ **Ride directly over the middle of the poles to ensure the distances in between them will still be perfect.**

Ride correctly up the center of the line. Frame your horse well with your aids, so he doesn't hit the poles. When you first approach this exercise and its many poles, you may feel a little daunted. However, with time and practice, you'll see just how much fun this can be. If you're at all unsure, begin this exercise in the posting trot.

This horse's tail carriage shows he's beginning to get tense. The rider can make a circle or other bending line to help him find relaxation again.

The first and last pole on the line should be placed straight and flat. As a final suggestion, ask a friend to join you for this one—riding such exercises in a group is even more fun for horses and riders!

### Solutions to Common Problems

**"My horse drifts left or right... now the distance between poles is no longer correct."**
- If your horse falls out, let's say to the right, you can help by framing him more with your aids on the right side. Keep those aids as you repeat Exercise 5.3 (p. 77) before trying this exercise again. In the meantime, you can also return to Exercise 2.2 (p. 20) to train your horse to activate his hindquarters and strengthen his shoulder girdle.

**Your Horse Has Mastered This Exercise—What's Next?**
➡ Choose between the next exercise in this chapter or begin with chapter 6.

## 5.5 The Long Line, Raised

*More work on coordination and concentration. We'll scale it back to 8 poles, but now we'll raise the poles on one side.*

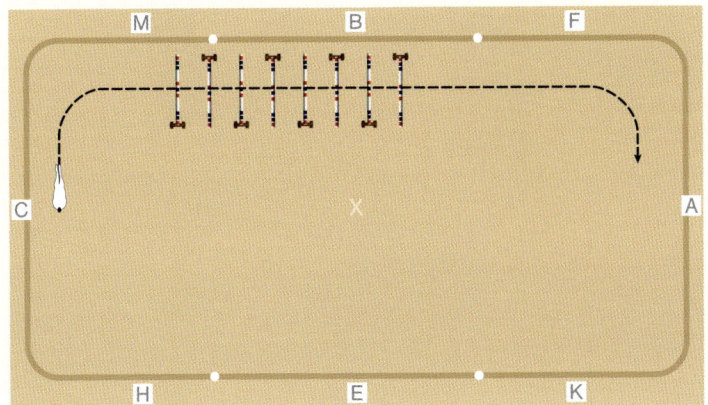

➡ **Make the distance between the poles just a bit wider than you have up to this point. Since we'll be asking the horse to lift his legs, his trot might get bigger. If the distance is left as it was or made smaller, we can start to improve the cadence.**

Place the poles along the third track, as shown in the diagram. Raise the poles on either the left or right side, alternating from one pole to the next.

Here, it's again important that you ride up the middle of the poles. For this exercise, the horse must lift his legs higher in order to avoid hitting the poles. This reinforces your training for his abdominals and back muscles, as well as his gluteal muscles. For this reason, it can be very strenuous work for the horse. Keep this in mind as you decide how often to repeat it.

### Solutions to Common Problems

**"My horse still always bumps a pole."**
- Are the distances between poles correct? Ask an assistant on the ground to help you check.

Go back to the prior exercises in this chapter to develop your horse's muscles further before you attempt this one again.

# POLE WORK FOR DRESSAGE RIDERS

The raised poles will challenge your horse to actively lift his legs. This will improve his ability to lower (flex) his hindquarters and thereby improve his trot.

**Your Horse Has Mastered This Exercise—What's Next?**

- Your horse has well-developed musculature and is well-trained. And how are you doing? Are you ready for exercises that demand more concentration and strength from the rider? Then I'd like to suggest you take a break from polework for at least two days before you move on to Exercise 6.1 (p. 84).
- In order to prepare for chapter 6 and stay motivated, you can start practicing with Exercise 2.3 (p. 22).

# 6. TROT POLES ON BENDING LINES

For the rider, pole exercises on bending lines are more difficult, since there's a constant need to guide the horse. However, from the horse's perspective, these exercises can be a bit easier. When he's in a bend, it's easier for his muscle groups to correctly contract and release over a long period of time. Exercises on a bending line will quickly reveal the horse's preferred side. For more info, refer to *Naturally Crooked or Nice and Straight?* (p. 56).

As you complete these exercises, make sure to weight your inside seat bone and drive the horse from your inside leg to your outside rein. Your outside leg holds and frames the horse. Your inside rein positions the horse, always softly giving and taking.

If your horse falls in and the circle is smaller than you'd like, you now know that his muscling on this side is insufficient to lift his shoulder correctly. This means his chest is twisting, and a crooked poll can also indicate this. In this case, refer to page 13 for more information on correct bend.

Support your horse with clear driving aids from your inside leg.

In order to strengthen the muscles that are lacking, I suggest you practice the exercises starting on page 19 in chapter 2, and/or revisit all of chapter 4.

You might also find that your horse wants to trot straight ahead and struggles to maintain the bending line. Or maybe he keeps making the circle bigger. In this case, by the end of the bending line, you're no longer crossing over the middle of the poles but finding yourself along the outside. This means your horse is finding it difficult to contract his muscles on the inside and stretch those along the outside. If this happens to you, I'd suggest you try Exercise 2.3 (p. 22). Use your outside rein to limit the horse. Often, the rider is not using the outside rein correctly.

Reminder 1: Take a break and then make sure to repeat the exercises in the second direction.

Reminder 2: Always measure your distances at the middle of the poles.

To prepare for the following exercises, it's wise to train all of the exercises in chapter 4. Doing so allows your horse to develop his musculature correctly while on the longe line.

## 6.1 The Quartet

*Before you begin practicing pole workouts that include bending lines, you need to start with the basics. Here, place four poles evenly spaced on a circle along the second arena track.*

# 6. Trot Poles on Bending Lines

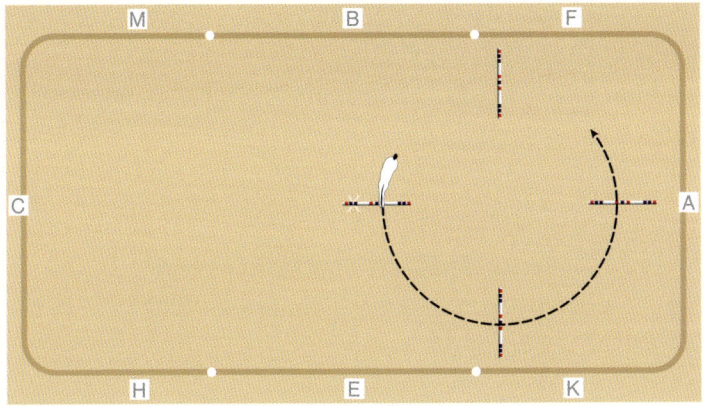

➡ *You can also use cavalletti. For this exercise, you'd want to use the lowest setting.*

Ride on a circle at the trot. Establish the right working tempo. Use a half-halt to prepare your horse. Ride over a pole, framing him with your aids in the way he's familiar with. The goal of this exercise is not necessarily to provide a workout that improves your horse's muscles; instead, it's a way of getting him familiar with pole work on bending lines. The rider is also learning how to frame the horse correctly, space the poles correctly, and correct the horse without causing stress should problems arise.

## Solutions to Common Problems

### "My horse falls to the inside and the circle keeps getting smaller."

- Ride the exercise like a square. As described above, your horse has contracted musculature and is demonstrating his crookedness. Return to the exercises beginning on page 19 in chapter 2 to strengthen his muscles. Make sure you're sitting on your inside seat bone and not turning too much to the inside.
- Seat errors can cause this problem, too. Make sure there's a give and take with your inside rein, and you're not just "hanging on it" under any circumstances.

### "My horse falls out and the circle keeps getting larger."

- Here, too, crookedness is the most likely culprit, whether the asymmetry originates with horse or rider. Begin with Exercise 2.3 (p. 22) to ensure your

POLE WORK FOR DRESSAGE RIDERS

basic steering aids are working well. Make sure to limit your horse with a quiet, steady outside rein.
- Read over *Naturally Crooked or Nice and Straight?* (p. 56).
- See chapter 4 for further ideas that can help here.

**Your Horse Has Mastered This Exercise—What's Next?**
➡ After a break, I recommend you continue training with the next exercise.

## 6.2 A Circle with Eight

*Now we'll try this exercise with four more poles. Place the poles as shown in the diagram. You can decide between a longer distance (2 to 4 strides) or a smaller distance, depending on how large a circle you plan to ride.*

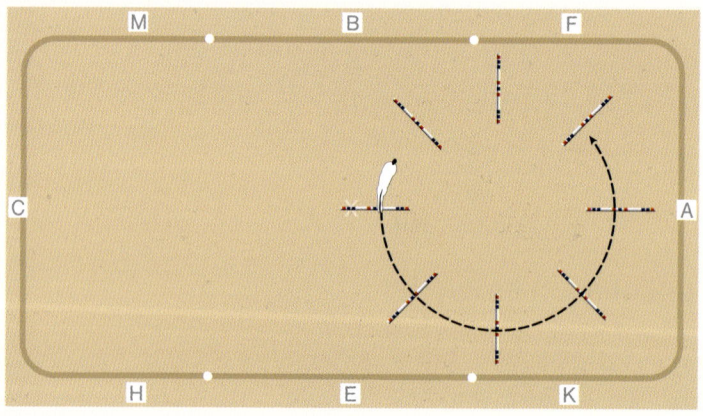

➡ *The bigger the circle, the easier it is for the horse.*

Ride on an even circle at the trot. You can choose to post the trot here. (Read over *Posting Trot Correctly*, p. 104.) Frame your horse with your aids and then don't bother him over the poles. Use your aids to steer when you're between the poles, not when you're riding over them. Use half-halts to keep your horse positioned and "on the aids"—always keep the goal of positive tension in mind.

## 6. Trot Poles on Bending Lines

Make sure you maintain a straight line from your elbow, through your hand, to the horse's mouth; this is what will allow you to execute your rein aids with refinement.

### Solutions to Common Problems

This exercise can also lead to some challenges. So I've compiled a list of issues and solutions you can explore.
- Horse falls in: Practice the exercises in *The Correct Bend* (p. 13).
- Horse falls out: Practice Exercise 2.3 (p. 22).
- Horse constantly hits a pole: Pay attention to which leg goes over the poles first. Repeat the exercise until he does it without hitting a pole and then praise him extensively, including the opportunity to stand and rest.
- This exercise works well in one direction, but not the other. In the difficult direction, we have one of the problems described above: Your horse's muscles have developed very differently on each side of his body. Try the corrective exercises offered above, repeating them more frequently in his "bad direction." Do this over several training sessions. If you find this doesn't improve the situation, I'd suggest you ask your horse's veterinarian or physical therapist for advice, and consult your own human bodyworker as well. It could be that either you or your horse have a physiological block.

**Your Horse Has Mastered This Exercise—What's Next?**
→ Take a break and then move onto Exercise 6.3 (p. 89).

1.
2.
3.
4.
5.
6.

In these photos, you can see the different phases of movement going over a line of poles. In the beginning of the exercise, the horse is a bit tense, which you can clearly see by his tail carriage. After the second pole, the tail is swinging again, and the musculature shows positive tone. This is a good thing, and should remain throughout the exercise and afterward. As your horse travels over the poles, try to stay relaxed. Breathe calmly and make sure to keep springiness in your ankle joints. Remember to keep your knee joint relaxed and sit up tall.

# 6.3 The Quartet in a Row

*Now we'll go back to just four poles. Place them near one another on the line of the circle; your horse will take just one stride in between each pole.*

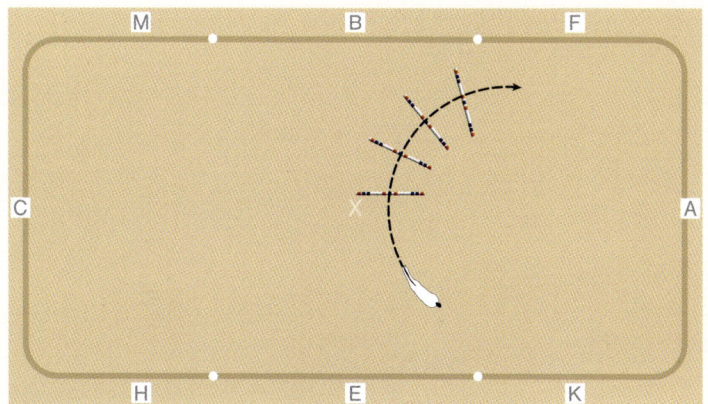

➡ **Count out loud: "1, 2, 1, 2, 1, 2..."**

Riding on the circle, establish a steady tempo at the trot. Travel over the poles. You'll notice it's more difficult to keep your horse on a bending line. As you ride, say out loud, "Pole, steer, pole, steer, etc." or, if you prefer, "1, 2, 1, 2, etc.," so you don't interfere with your horse when he's trotting over the poles. Stay on the line of the circle, until your horse can complete this exercise at an even tempo and without error. Then praise your horse extensively!

## Solutions to Common Problems

### "My horse likes to suck back and fall to the inside."
- In contrast to the solutions presented in the book thus far, you might try looking toward the outside end of the poles here, rather than looking out and over the last pole. Stretch tall through the inside of your body and apply your inside leg to prevent the horse from falling in.
- Use half-halts to prepare your horse. Always keep in mind the correct positioning of his movement centers.

POLE WORK FOR DRESSAGE RIDERS

**Your Horse Has Mastered This Exercise—What's Next?**
➡ I suggest you take a break and then give the next exercise a try.

## 6.4 High Up—Part 1

Now it's time to dig deep and get started with the real workout! Place 8 poles, one after another, on a circle. Raise four poles at the outside ends. In the diagram, you can see how every other pole is raised at the outside. A tip: Use the third arena track for this exercise.

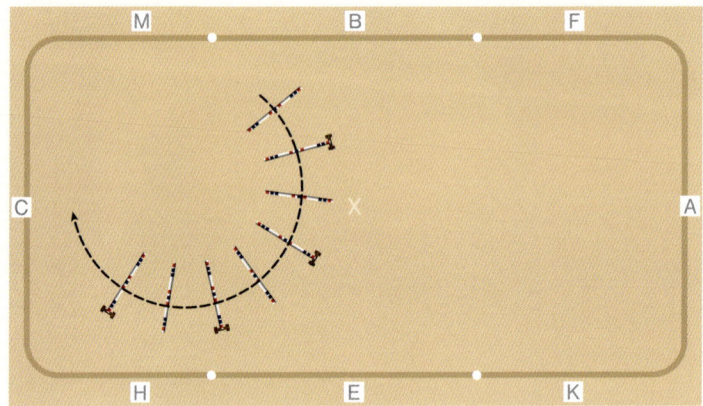

➡ *If your horse trots over the first pole with his inside foreleg, it will be easier for him to get around the poles with a correct bend and without hitting any poles.*

### Solutions to Common Problems

#### "My horse always hits one..."
- Make sure you're following loosely with your hips. Take note of which leg needs to make it over the raised end of the poles. Repeat the exercise until your horse can do it without hitting a pole. Then allow him to come to a stop and praise him extensively.
- Another thought—are your poles spaced correctly? Try riding over the poles a bit further to the outside or the inside. Your horse may need the distance between the poles adjusted, now that one end is raised.

6. Trot Poles on Bending Lines

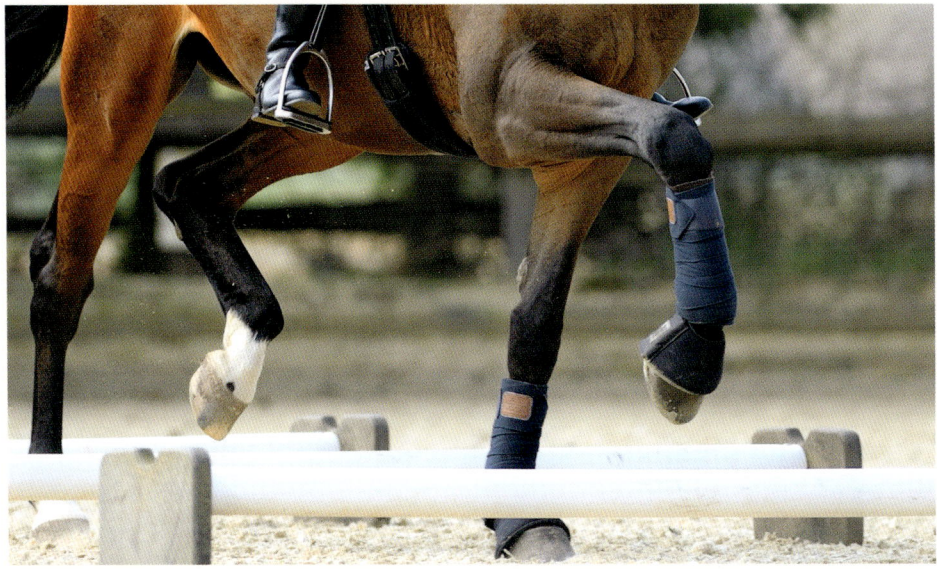

Here, the horse could be a bit more active with his hind leg as he lifts it up and forwards. He's not lowering his hindquarters correctly yet. Support your horse with forward driving leg aids to help him trot more actively. In turn, this will lift his back and make it easier for you to follow his movement.

Practice this exercise over a longer period of time before you move onto the next one.

### Wow, You Did It! Awesome!
➡ Now you can take it one step further with the next exercise.

## 6.5 High Up—Part 2

*Place eight poles in a row, including one or two raised at the outside end, at the inside end, or both outside and inside. I suggest you use the third arena track. You can also use more than eight poles, but make sure you don't overdo it with your horse.*

➡ **Make sure you ride an even circle.**

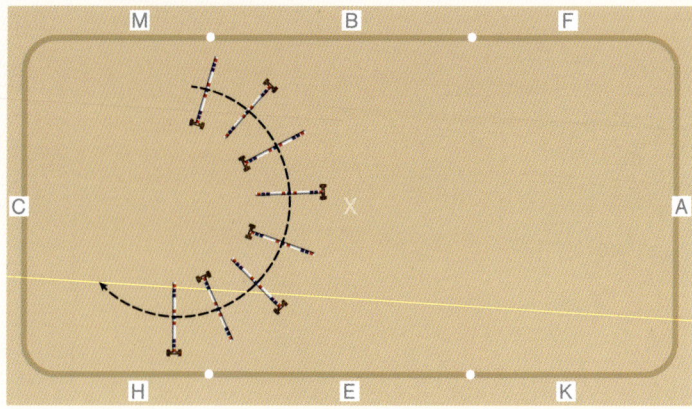

Stay on the circle over the poles until you're ready to conclude the exercise. For your horse, it's much easier to get over the poles if you maintain a consistent circle radius. If you wish, you can add a couple of cones to help establish the line of travel along the circle, which gives both you and your horse a visual barrier.

As soon as your horse crosses over all the poles successfully, praise him extensively! He's done really good work and has more than earned your praise. A walk break can help—make sure you allow him to chew the reins from your hands as he stretches out.

### Solutions to Common Problems

- In this exercise, you may encounter many of the same challenges that have already been discussed in the prior exercises.
- Take your time reading through previously suggested solutions—you can use those to resolve your current issues.
- Repeat this exercise over a longer period of time before you move onto the next exercises.

**Your Horse Has Mastered This Exercise—Wow, Impressive!**
  ➡ Your horse has developed good musculature and is well-trained. Now you can get creative and begin combining multiple exercises, or try out the combinations included in the next chapter.

# 7. COMBINATIONS

There are many roads that lead to Rome. Therefore, you can get creative about how you combine the poles. The correct distance is always important. Make sure you and your horse stay motivated and ready to try new things.

There are no limits to your imagination.

When starting with combinations, it's important to build on your previous work. Before you begin the following exercises, your horse should already be confident in his work over poles on straight lines and curved lines. The following exercises require a lot of muscular strength.

There are many possibilities and creative ways to set up combinations. In order to find the correct combinations for your horse, it's important to consider your horse's current level of training.

Build on your experience with the previous exercises and tips when coming up with combinations. Here's what is most important to keep in mind:

If your horse has a **low level of training** or needs to develop more strength and endurance, the first two exercises in the previous chapters may have worked well for you.

In this case, you should not set up more than four poles per line as part of a combination. Leave enough space between each line of poles to allow your horse to recover and come back to your aids. You can also use the more difficult exercises in this chapter—just be mindful and design your combination in such a way that your horse has enough time to take a break between short lines of poles. Expand the number of short lines gradually over the course of several weeks.

Moving over **diagonally positioned poles** requires coordination from your horse, and you should be able to ride in a frame easily. Don't raise diagonally positioned poles!

Working over **poles that are raised on both sides**, or cavalletti on a low setting, requires a higher level of training for your horse. These exercises improve cadence and activate the ventral muscle chain. The hindquarters drop lower, and the forehand has to rise. The horse should easily go in a frame and be straight. The goals for these exercises are mostly conditioning and muscle development.

**Poles that are raised on one side, alternating sides,** help the horse find the center of the poles by creating a visual effect of crossing when viewed from the front.

# 7. Combinations

Keeping the horse in a frame is much easier. They serve as good transitional exercises between poles on the ground and poles that are raised on both sides.

**Poles that are raised on the outside** help the horse lift the outside shoulder. The outside shoulder girdle is strengthened and therefore helps the horse achieve straightness. This is a good exercise to support straightness in your horse, and a good schooling method for horses who push to the outside. To learn more about this topic, read the section *Naturally Crooked or Nice and Straight?* (p. 56).

In conjunction with a thorough analysis of your horse and the associated training tools, these combinations can infuse fun into your training and turn into a real pole workout for the horse. Still, challenges may arise. Since many of the difficulties will fall into certain broad categories, I am presenting the most common ones and their solutions here.

When you encounter problems with the exercises, try switching to an easier exercise or reducing the number of poles. You can also practice the exercises without any raised poles, and once your horse has mastered that variation, add raised poles back into your training.

Please don't overwhelm your horse! Build in many breaks. Breaks make the most sense after your horse has performed an exercise correctly—this way, your horse will stay motivated.

Horses are creatures of habit. Repeat the exercises often and revisit the same exercise again and again. Even once you've read and practiced all exercises in this book, your horse will benefit greatly from revisiting the very first exercises. Don't switch up the exercises every day. If your horse has difficulty mastering long lines of poles, reduce the number of poles you are using, or jump back to earlier chapters in the book and focus on conditioning and developing your horse's musculature.

If your horse falls to the outside consistently, you may not be framing your horse with the outside aids correctly, you may sit crookedly, or your horse may need support such as raising the poles at the outside ends.

If your horse falls to the inside, your inside leg may not provide enough support. Maybe the horse is trying to evade work, or needs more support from your inside leg. In this case, you should raise the poles at the inside end.

If your horse speeds up between the pole lines, his musculature may be lacking. Often horses are unable to use their musculature effectively over a longer period of time, and as a result they will fall on to the forehand. In order to make it over the poles, the hind end is raised or tensed, and the horse speeds up. Here, too, it's important to raise the level of difficulty slowly. Help your horse with half-halts and sufficient breaks for recovery time.

These combinations are the most fun to practice with somebody else or in a bigger group. Setup and breakdown are quicker, and you can help each other. Make sure levels of training aren't too different across the group.

## 7.1 Combo 1

*This combination consists of straight and bending lines. Position the poles in the middle of the arena as indicated in the diagram. This exercise can be done in the walk or trot.*

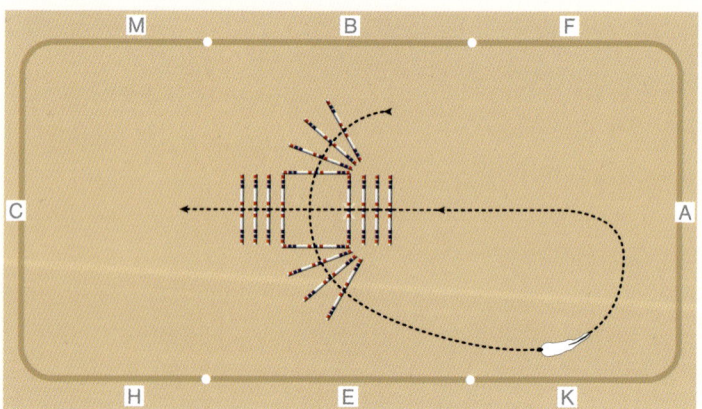

➡ **Make sure to choose the correct distances for the chosen gait.**

To make this exercise more difficult, you can raise the poles on the straight line on both sides or on one side.

7. Combinations

If you choose to work with raised poles, the first and last poles need to be flat on the ground.

## Which Exercises Should You Have Mastered Before Starting This Exercise?
- All the walk and trot exercises on straight and bending lines.

## Your Horse Has Mastered This Exercise—What's Next?
I recommend that after a break you continue with the following exercises:
- ➡ This exercise, repeated with raised poles or cavalletti.
- ➡ The next combination exercise, integrating changes of direction.
- ➡ Improve transitions and rhythm.

# 7.2 Combo 2 with a Change of Direction

*This combination consists of straight lines and bending lines, and also includes changes of direction. Position the poles as shown in the diagram, in the middle of the arena. This exercise can be ridden in the trot or walk. Be mindful of the distances between poles, depending on your chosen gait.*

# POLE WORK FOR DRESSAGE RIDERS

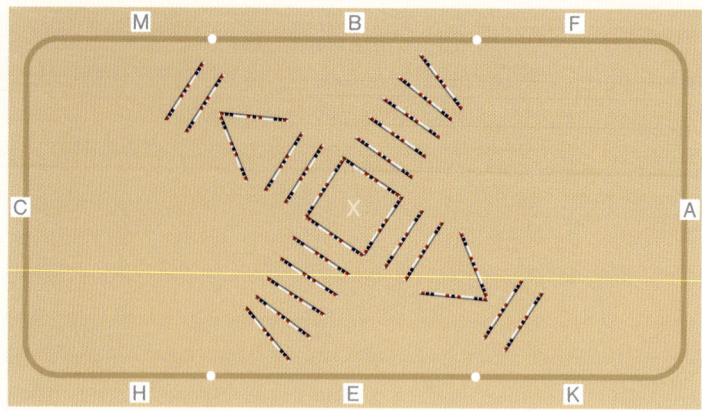

➡ **Professionals can ride this setup in the canter with flying changes, if the distances between the poles are correct.**

Similar to Exercise 7.1, this setup is focused on straight lines and bending lines, but it adds frequent changes of direction. Use half-halts to prepare your horse for the changes from straight lines to bending lines and the changes of direction. You can make this exercise more challenging by raising both sides of the poles. Raising just one side of the poles on the bending lines can improve the horse's straightness.

## Which Exercises Should You Have Mastered Before Starting This Exercise?
- All walk and trot exercises on straight lines and bending lines.
- Exercise 7.1 (p. 96).
- If you're working in the canter, I recommend working through chapters 8 and 9 first.

## Your Horse Has Mastered This Exercise—What's Next?
I recommend that after a break you continue with the following exercises:
  ➡ This exercise, repeated with raised poles or cavalletti.
  ➡ Improve transitions and rhythm.

7. Combinations

Here you can clearly see that horse and rider are enjoying this exercise. The horse's musculature is well developed, and the exercise seems easy. Now is the time to progress to the next exercise.

## 7.3 Improving Transitions and Rhythm

*As the name of this combination indicates, our focus is now on transitions and correct rhythm. The diagram is meant to be done in walk and trot. Be mindful of the distances between the poles.*

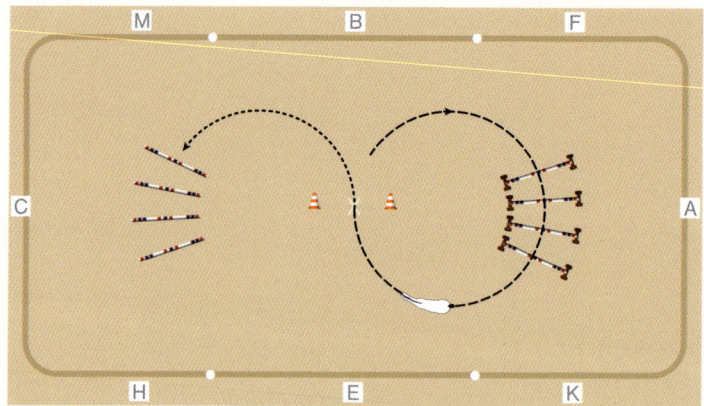

➡ **Choose the size of your circles carefully—make them big enough for your horse to maintain the correct rhythm.**

Position 2 cones in the middle of the arena, as indicated in the diagram. Now put 4 poles on one side of the figure-eight, set apart at trot distances, and 4 poles on the other side, set apart at walk distances. Now ride the figure-eight, and choose the new direction and gait between the two cones.

### Which Exercises Should You Have Mastered Before Starting This Exercise?
- Exercise 3.3 (p. 39).
- Exercise 6.3 (p. 89).

### Your Horse Has Mastered This Exercise—What's Next?
Take a break and then continue with the following exercises:
  ➡ All trot and walk exercises.
  ➡ Exercise 7.4 (p. 101).
  ➡ Exercise 7.5 (p. 102).

# 7.4 Side and High

*This exercise lifts the sternum, opens the thigh musculature, and bends the hocks. A great exercise that requires you and your horse to have mastered the leg yield or half pass.*

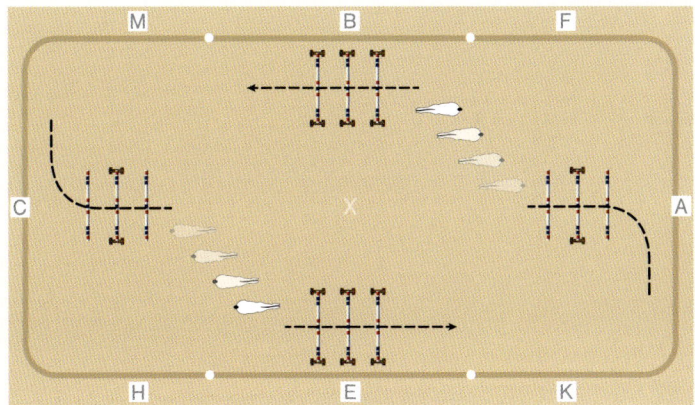

➡ **You can raise the poles or cavalletti according to the level of difficulty.**

Place the poles in the arena as shown in the diagram. Turn on to the centerline in a trot over the poles, and leg yield or half pass right away until you reach the third track. Ideally you will reach the raised poles after four or five steps. Once you cross the poles, turn back on to the center line. Change direction often by riding the leg yield or half pass alternating between the left and the right.

## Which Exercises Should You Have Mastered Before Starting This Exercise?
- Leg yield or half pass should be mastered.
- Exercise 5.1 (p. 73).

If you ride the exercise correctly, you'll experience a lifting forehand and improved cadence.

Make sure the poles or cavalletti aren't spaced too far apart. A helper on the ground can adjust the distances.

### Your Horse Has Mastered This Exercise—What's Next?

I recommend that you continue after a break with the following exercises:

➡ All trot exercises.

➡ The next exercise.

➡ Tempo changes within the gaits—jump to chapter 11.

## 7.5 Every Which Way

*Place the poles as shown in the diagram and ride the marked lines. Or you can place the poles wherever you please.*

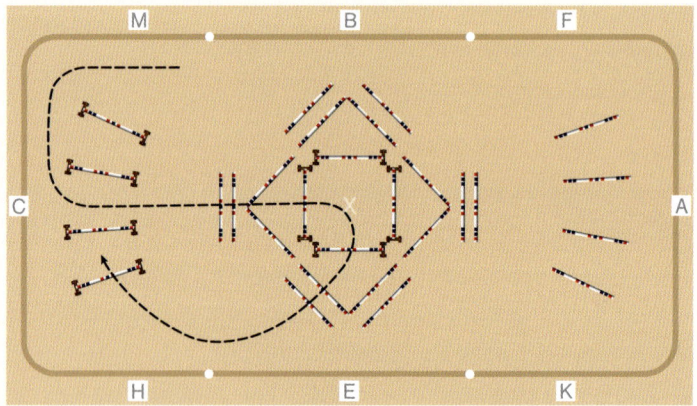

➡ ***This exercise is most fun when done as a group!***

You can mix and match combinations as you please, and place poles wherever you like. However, it's important to plan your lines before you start riding, and to make sure the distances between poles match the gait you choose. Walk the lines on foot before you ride. The earlier exercises will have taught you which exercises have which effect. Ask yourself the following questions when setting up the poles: What does my horse need? So far, which exercises have had what effect? Is my horse straight or does he still need support?

# 7. Combinations

## Which Exercises Should You Have Mastered Before Starting This Exercise?

- You should have mastered trot poles on straight and bending lines.

This exercise offers many different lines. Try out all possible combinations before continuing with the next structured exercise.

**The different lines:**

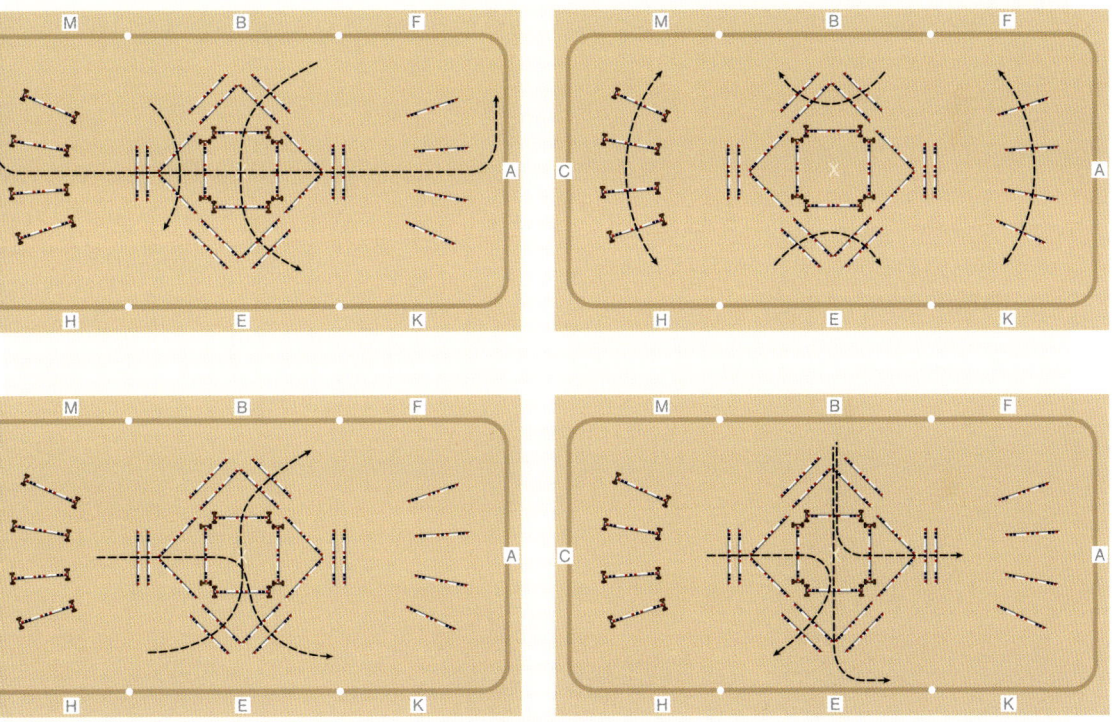

## Your Horse Has Mastered This Exercise—What's Next?

⇒ After being colorful and creative, you can now return to more structured exercises. Continue with the next exercise—just turn the page.

# SIDE NOTE: POSTING TROT CORRECTLY

Up and down—you may think that shouldn't be too difficult. But correct posting isn't easy. Again and again, you'll see desperate riders in the arena trying to execute the "jumping jack" correctly: standing up using the stirrups, which move far away from the horse's barrel in the process, just to sit back down in the saddle (gently, of course), while at the same time poking the heels into the horse's body to prevent the horse from stopping altogether.

But how do you post correctly, and what are the origins of posting?

In the 18th century, it was necessary to quickly prepare inexperienced soldiers to ride into war. At the same time, aristocrats in England learned posting, since many were not accomplished riders and needed to stay on their horses at high tempo during hunting. Therefore, posting was also known as "English trotting."

Nowadays, posting is mostly used during the warm-up phase. In the process, the inside hind is supposed to be activated and encouraged to reach forward, to allow it to carry increased weight. In order to activate the horse's inside hind leg, the rider's inside leg needs to squeeze simultaneously with the inside foot leaving the ground. When the rider rises as the horse's inside hind comes forward, it makes an increased forward swing of the inside hind leg possible, while at the same time taking weight off the horse's back.

➡ ***In short: The rider should, while standing up, encourage the inside hind leg to step forward.***

But is this communicated in lesson programs? Most of the time, unfortunately, no, since it's much harder than the "jumping jack method."

In order to post correctly and use the forward moving aids correctly, it is first of all important not to rise up any higher than necessary. This is much easier if the upper body of the rider is leaning forward slightly. The knees need to stay bent during the rising phase, making it possible for the lower leg to effectively move the horse forward. When rising, the rider should only move her hips forward. The "rising" is initiated by the horse's movement.

Correct posting can warm up and supple the horse, and it can help to improve rhythm. But incorrect posting has a negative effect on rhythm, relaxation, and the back musculature of the horse. In addition, too much posting can block the hip joint of the rider, making it impossible for the rider to move with the horse's movement with feeling in the sitting trot anymore. I highly encourage you to learn correct posting, possibly through seat training on the longe line.

7. Combinations

Aline's upper body is leaning forward slightly, helping the young stallion to eagerly move forward and loosening his musculature.

---

Later on in the warm-up phase, Aline positions her upper body further back. Here you can see how Don Charlton shows more self-carriage and his hind end is starting to carry more weight.

Here, the horse is bent too much to the inside. The rider's hip is folding, and the horse is tense in the neck and shoulder areas.

In this picture, too, the rider is folding in her hip joint, albeit lightly, and the inside hand is not relaxed, carried in front of her, but appears tense and stiff. Compared to the positive tension shown in the previous images, there's a clear difference in the horse—a bracing tension, instead. The area of the shoulder and neck is tight, and the forehand is not moving as freely.

If you run into problems when relearning correct posting, you can try posting on the "wrong" diagonal. This allows for forward moving aids in the correct moment, but it doesn't ease the weight on the horse's back while the inside leg swings forward. Still, it has an effect on your horse. It is most important to be able to feel when and how the horse moves his feet in order to correct and activate the horse at the exact right moment.

In order to feel this movement, it's not only necessary to practice for years, but to be able to freely follow the horse's movement from the middle of the body.

Read *A Centered, Supple Position* (p.35).

Observing riders in the sitting trot, too, there are often wobbly legs, bumping into the horse's belly unintentionally every half second.

# SIDE NOTE: HALF-HALTS AND FULL HALTS

As you probably already know, the half-halt is a combination of all aids. A full halt always leads to a halt. So far, so good. But why? And what exactly is the purpose?

Let's try to analyze the 1–2 seconds of a half-halt in slow motion. We can distinguish 6 phases. During Phase 1, the positive tension of the rider is increased. During Phase 2, the forehand is directed forward with the help of the legs and weight of the rider. During Phase 3, the forehand is lifted by using holding rein and weight aids. In Phase 4, the hind end is closed through forward moving weight and leg aids, and in Phase 5, the horse's positive body tension is elevated. During Phase 6, the correct self-carriage of the horse is being checked by giving the reins.

This explains why the half-halt is not only important for transitions and to prepare for a new exercise, but is also essential in order for the horse to use his center of movement correctly and to ensure an uphill movement.

During the full halt, the same phases occur; however, Phase 4 includes not only the closing of the hind end, but at the same time a closing of the forehand with the help of weight and rein aids, which leads to a full halt. If this phase is executed correctly, the horse will stand square, and positive tension works in opposition to gravity. The result is a horse who is on the aids and can move off the slightest aids in the desired gait.

In the arena, you often hear the term "playing." But what does it mean, and is "playing" part of the half halt?

The term "playing" describes the subtle impulse in the horse's mouth that is initiated by a soft shortening and lengthening of the rein. This causes the fascia from the mouth to the neck to relax, since the impulse encourages the horse to chew—just like with children who are offered chewing gum to relax their musculature and jaw joint. Through the chewing movement, the fascia and muscles relax. Relaxation works to counter negative tension, and improves concentration and performance. Among other results, this leads to positive tension in the horse's body.

# 7.6 The Simple Serpentine

*This arena pattern is probably very familiar to you. Position the poles as shown in the diagram along the line of the arena figure.*

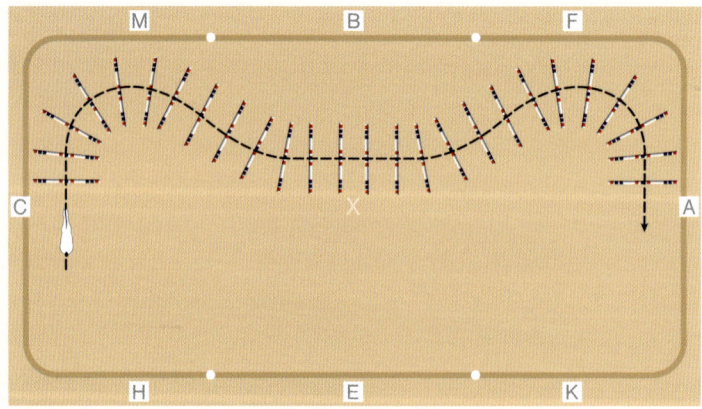

➡ **Change your horse's bend at the correct point.**

Ride around the whole arena in the trot. Start at A or C. I recommend posting. Don't emphasize your rise, but rather your sit, in order to avoid your horse getting too fast and ensure that your horse stays in a good frame.

Prepare the change of diagonal well with half halts. Read *Posting Trot Correctly* (p. 104) and *Half-Halts and Full Halts* (p. 107).

## Which Exercises Should You Have Mastered Before Starting This Exercise?
- The serpentine arena figure should be well-known to you and your horse.
- All exercises on curved lines in the trot.

## Your Horse Has Mastered This Exercise—What's Next?
I recommend that you continue after a break with the following exercises:
  ➡ The next exercise.
  ➡ Exercise 7.8 (p. 110).

# 7.7 Change across the Long Diagonal

*This exercise combines straight and bending lines. Position the poles as shown in the diagram, starting at A or C and then along the diagonal.*

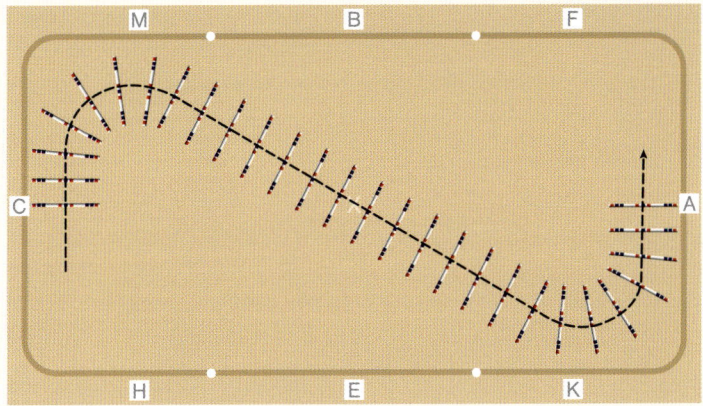

➡ **Set up the exercise alternating from M to K or from F to H, so that you can practice both changes of direction.**

If this exercise is too difficult, or if you don't have enough poles, you can make your setup smaller, or only put out every other pole shown in the diagram.

Having said that, this exercise has a great impact if you can set it up and ride it as shown in the diagram. Maybe you can find a few poles somewhere. Ride around the whole arena in the trot. Start at A or C. I recommend posting. Don't emphasize the rising phase of your post, but rather the sitting phase, in order to avoid your horse speeding up too much and ensure he stays in a good frame. Prepare for the change of direction well with half-halts. Review *Posting Trot Correctly* (p. 104) and *Half-Halts and Full Halts* (p. 107).

### Which Exercises Should You Have Mastered Before Starting This Exercise?
- Exercises 6.1 to 6.3 (pp. 84-89).
- All exercises in chapters 4 and 5.

### Your Horse Has Mastered This Exercise—What's Next?
I recommend that you continue after a break with the following exercises:
- Additional exercises from this chapter.
- Exercises from chapters 8 or 10.

# 7.8 Serpentines

*You're probably very familiar with this arena pattern. In this exercise, the difficulty lies in the multiple changes of direction that occur while riding over the poles. This means your horse has to be securely on the aids. Prepare for each change of direction with a half-halt. This exercise doesn't just improve rhythm, it has an impact on all muscles in the horse's body.*

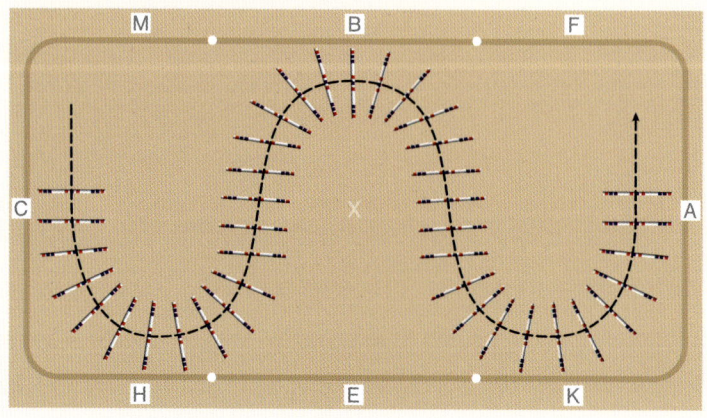

7. Combinations

➡ *You can set up every other pole shown in the diagram, if you don't have enough poles.*

Ride around the whole arena in the trot. Start at A or C. I recommend posting. Once again, emphasize the sitting phase of your post, in order to avoid your horse getting too fast and to ensure that your horse stays in a good frame. Prepare the change of direction well with half halts.

## Which Exercises Should You Have Mastered Before Starting This Exercise?
- You should have mastered the basic serpentine arena figure.
- Exercise 7.6 (p. 108).
- Exercise 7.7 (p. 109).

## Your Horse Has Mastered This Exercise—What's Next?
I recommend that you continue after a break with the following exercises:
➡ The next exercise.
➡ A new chapter.

# 7.9 Infinity Loop

*This exercise requires muscle strength and endurance. For this exercise, you can evenly space the poles over the whole 20-meter circle. You can partially raise the poles, too, which will increase the level of difficulty.*

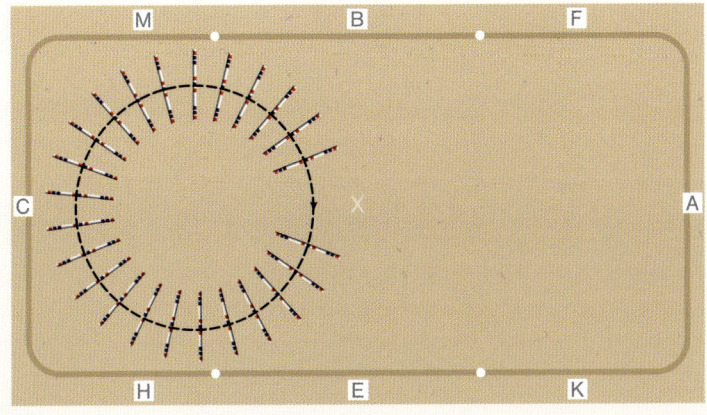

➡ *Leave a space at X so you can enter or exit any time.*

You are familiar with this setup from chapter 4. Now, however, it's not only your horse that has to master this exercise; you will be challenged to do so as well. This continuous loop can be intimidating to some riders—it's one of the most challenging exercises in this book. Start by setting up every other pole, and refrain from raising any poles.

Once you overcome your fear and you and your horse move through this exercise as a unit, you will observe how every muscle in your horse's body is engaged.

Build in breaks for your horse! And be mindful of the change of direction. This exercise can be revisited over the course of many weeks. Please allow for sufficient recovery time for your horse between training sessions. To begin with, this exercise can be ridden once a week. Later on, two to three times a week. But please don't overwhelm your horse!

## Which Exercises Should You Have Mastered Before Starting This Exercise?
- Previous exercises in this chapter.
- All exercises in chapter 4.

## Your Horse Has Mastered This Exercise—What's Next?
I recommend that you continue, after a break, with the following exercises:
➡ The next exercise.
➡ The exercises in chapter 8.

# 7.10 Figure Eight

*You and your horse know how to change direction by moving from one circle to another. Now poles will be distributed around those two circles, and you'll continuously move from one circle to the other. This exercise is one of the most challenging in this book—it requires a lot of muscle strength and endurance.*

➡ *Leave enough space at X to allow time for the change of direction.*

# 7. Combinations

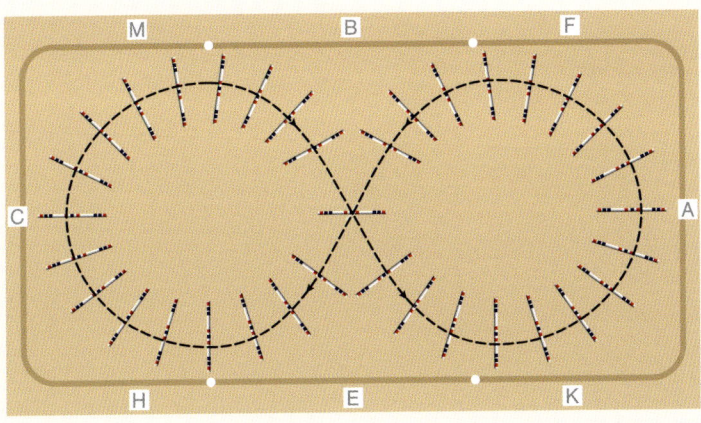

You can set up this exercise with many variations, including raising different poles either on one side or on both sides.

Don't start this exercise before you master Exercise 7.9. Once the Infinity Loop works well, you won't be afraid of this figure-eight. If you're still a little intimidated, start by setting up every other pole shown in the diagram, and refrain from raising any poles.

Build in breaks for your horse!

This exercise can be revisited over the course of many weeks. Please allow for sufficient recovery time for your horse between training sessions. To begin with, this exercise can be ridden once a week. Later on, two to three times a week. But once again, please don't overwhelm your horse.

## Which Exercises Should You Have Mastered Before Starting This Exercise?
- Exercise 7.9 (p. 111).
- All exercises in chapter 4.

## Your Horse Has Mastered This Exercise—What's Next?
- ➡ Wow! You've put in a lot of time and effort to ensure your horse develops strong, healthy muscles. I recommend you take a break, and then continue with the exercises in the next chapter.

# 8. CANTER EXERCISES ON THE LONGE

# 8. Canter Exercises on the Longe

In this chapter, we will explore canter poles on the longe line. This will help with training your eye and learning to analyze your horse's movement. Especially for explosive horses and insecure riders, it can be helpful to do canter work on the longe line.

Canter poles and trot poles improve rhythm and musculature in your horse. The forehand gets lighter and the hind end lowers. The canter workout starts on the longe line to allow the horse to learn to canter correctly over the poles. As soon as your horse has developed enough strength, you can start riding the exercises in this chapter and the next.

Even assuming that the distances between the poles are correctly measured for your horse, the following mistakes can still occur.

## Common Mistakes and Their Solutions

- **Splitting the poles:** One of the front or hind legs lands behind the pole, while the other stays on the ground in front of the pole. For a brief moment, the pole ends up not between the forehand and hindquarters, but between the left and right front or hind legs.
- **Diving:** The distance between front legs and pole is too great. The horse must adjust by taking a very big canter stride. The rhythm is lost, and the horse has difficulty staying balanced.
- **Too close:** The horse's front legs are too close to the pole. He has to make a short jump before finding his natural rhythm again.
- **Too far to the outside:** As the horse moves on a larger circle or pushes to the outside, the distances are incorrect, since they are always measured at the center of the pole.
- **Too far to the inside:** The horse travels on a smaller circle or falls in. The distances between the poles decrease and a correct rhythm is not possible anymore.

To avoid these mistakes, begin with Exercise 8.1 (p. 118). This exercise can be ridden to train the eye and get familiar with distances. The following pictures of possible mistakes will help you train your eye.

Here the horse moved too close to the pole, possibly stepping on it. Choose a larger circle to make the distances and your horse's canter strides match.

Compared to the first picture, the horse in the second picture is cantering further to the outside of the circle and the distances fit better.

## 8. Canter Exercises on the Longe

In the third picture the size of the circle was chosen correctly. After the pole the horse maintains a correct canter stride.

Here you can see clearly that the whip did not correctly frame the horse and as a result he dives over the pole with a slight bend to the outside. Frame your horse with the whip and stay standing in the middle of the circle to allow the horse to canter around you smoothly.

## 8.1 How to Begin

*To begin working in the canter, you can start with 4 poles on a circle. Set up 8 cones in front of and behind the poles. The cones should be set apart at the same distance as the poles—9–10 feet (3 meters).*

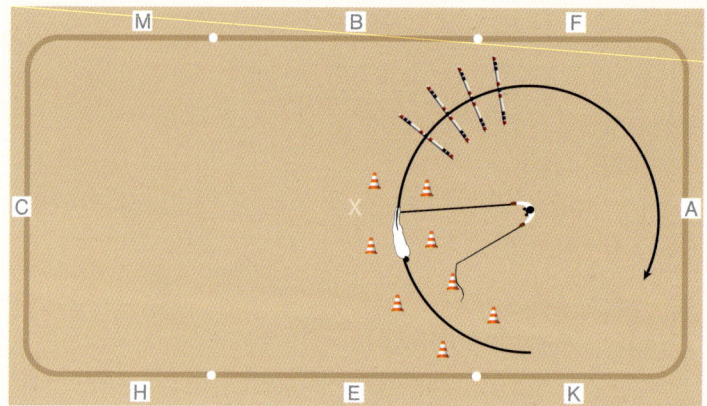

➡ **Use the cones to longe your horse over the center of the poles with good rhythm. As soon as you and your horse have learned to get over the poles without making any mistakes, you can reduce the number of cones (see below).**

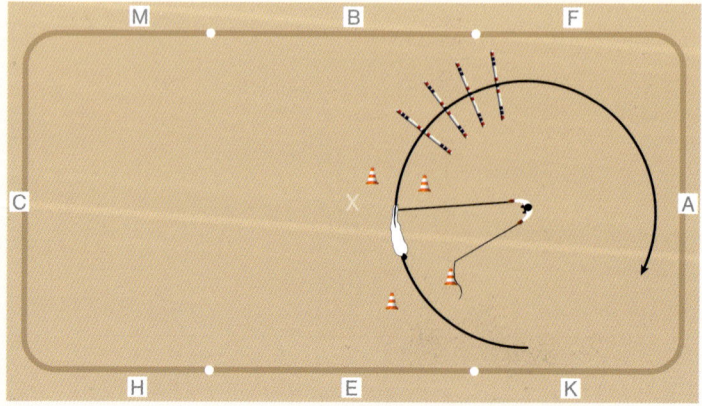

# 8. Canter Exercises on the Longe

The tension in the horse clearly shows he hasn't developed enough strength to maintain a regular rhythm over the poles in the canter. In this case, start in small steps and increase the level of difficulty only once your horse stays relaxed and the workout appears easy for him.

Start by longeing your horse over the poles in the trot. The horse should step into the distances between the poles and cones with both front legs. If the distances don't fit his strides or he has to change rhythm when he gets to the poles, you should correct the distances.

As soon as the rhythm in the trot is even and smooth, transition your horse to a canter and let him go over the poles. Again, the horse should step into the space between the poles and cones with his front legs first, followed by his hind legs.

An important goal of this exercise is for you and your horse to learn to estimate distances. By the time you're around 20–30 feet (6–9 meters) in front of the first pole, you'll already be able to tell whether the distance is going to be correct. Should the distances not be correct, you can change the size of the circle you're longeing on or the distances between the poles. Remember to change direction often.

Once you can use your trained eye to longe your horse over the poles without any mistakes, while maintaining good rhythm, you can begin with the next exercise.

# POLE WORK FOR DRESSAGE RIDERS

The side-reins should be longer when set low on the surcingle to allow the horse to stretch, or they need to be connected higher on the surcingle to allow the horse to bring his head in front of the vertical.

## 8.2 Tempo and Rhythm

*To find the correct rhythm in the canter, we will begin with 6 poles on the circle line. The poles are raised, alternating between the inside and outside ends.*

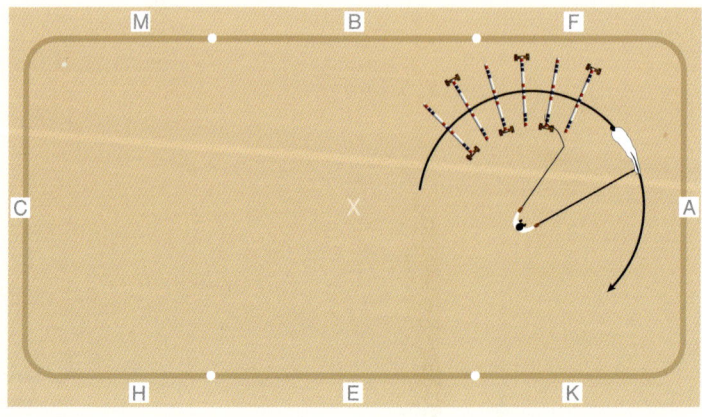

## 8. Canter Exercises on the Longe

➡ **To help your horse find the center of the poles, the poles should be raised at one end, alternating between the inside and outside ends.**

Begin by longeing your horse over the poles in the trot. As soon as the rhythm in the trot is even and smooth, transition to canter and longe him over the poles in the canter. The even, smooth canter should be maintained before, over, and after each pole. The previous exercise prepared you to longe your horse toward the poles correctly, avoiding any diving or splitting and making sure the horse doesn't canter too far out or too far in over the first pole.

### Solutions to Common Problems

**"My horse loses his rhythm."**
- Despite all your effort, it's possible the distances between the poles don't work for your horse. Bring a helper with you to the arena, who can adjust the poles if necessary.

**"My horse pulls to the outside."**
- I highly recommend making use of a longeing ring, if you have access to one. If not, you can use other means to create an outside barrier until your horse has learned to move on the circle line.

### Your Horse Has Mastered This Exercise—What's Next?
➡ Make sure you and your horse both feel comfortable with this exercise in both directions. Then, I'd suggest you take a break before moving on to the next exercise. Or you can try this and the previous exercise under saddle. Read *Canter Aids on Bending Lines* (p. 130).

## 8.3 Double In-Out

*This exercise encourages horses to lift the forehand and extend the time they support their weight on one leg. Set up three cavalletti on opposite sides of the circle on their highest or medium setting.*

## POLE WORK FOR DRESSAGE RIDERS

Don Charlton jumps the very inside of the pole into the in-out, which leads him to overcorrect by pulling to the outside in the following picture. Choose an appropriate center for your circle and stay there while your horse is cantering around you. This way you avoid shifting the circle, and your horse will approach the cavalletti correctly.

# 8. Canter Exercises on the Longe

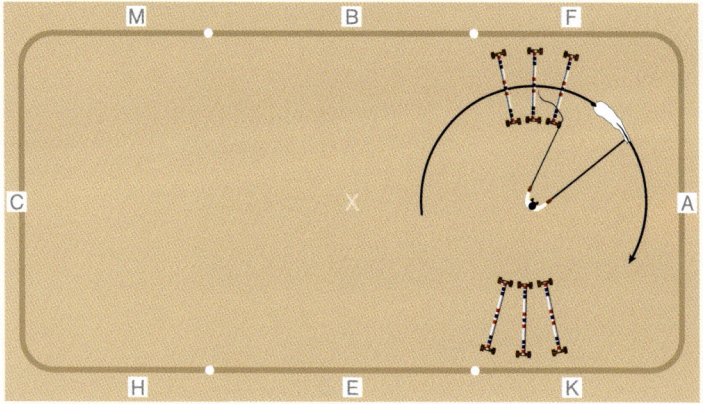

➡ *When using a longeing ring, you can measure the distances at the outer third of the poles, rather than the middle. This will allow your horse to canter on the outside track.*

Start by longeing your horse next to the cavalletti until he finds a steady rhythm. Now let him canter over the cavalletti. For this exercise, it's necessary for the horse to canter over the middle of the cavalletti.

➡ *Important! Don't use side-reins for this exercise.*

As soon as you observe your horse cantering with a correct top line over the in-out, rather than jumping in an exaggerated way, you've achieved the goal of this exercise.

### Solutions to Common Problems

**"My horse pulls up his head again and again."**
- Practice this exercise repeatedly over a longer period. Your horse must develop an idea of how to use his musculature correctly for this exercise.

### Your Horse Has Mastered This Exercise—What's Next?
➡ Make sure you and your horse both feel comfortable with this exercise in both directions. Then, I'd suggest you take a break before moving on to the next exercise.

## 8.4 Canter Workout

*Now let's continue with the canter workout. Set up cavalletti, ground poles, and poles raised on one end on the circle. This exercise helps develop belly, legs, back, and hind end musculature.*

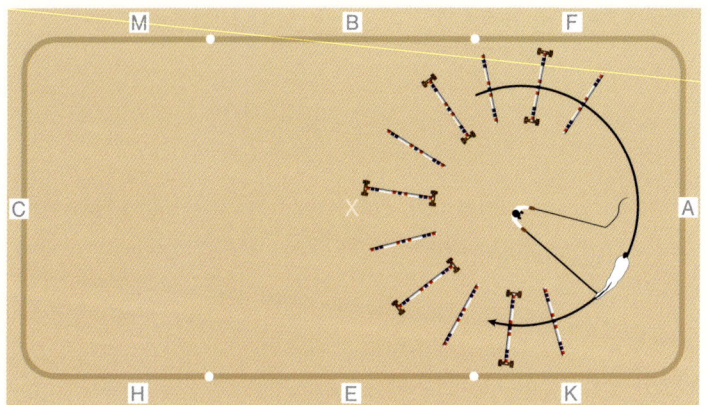

➡ **The more variation in height you include in this exercise, the more challenging and effective it will be.**

Start by longeing your horse next to the cavalletti and poles until he finds a steady rhythm. Now let him canter over the cavalletti and poles. The horse must canter over the middle of the cavalletti.

➡ **Important: Only use side-reins after consulting your trainer! At a certain height, you should forgo the use of side-reins entirely.**

Prerequisites for this exercise include all the earlier exercises in this chapter, in addition to all exercises in chapter 4.

### Solutions to Common Problems

- The variations in height can cause your horse to become quick and hectic. Think through your setup and adjust it to the level of training of your horse.

8. Canter Exercises on the Longe

For example, you can use the medium setting for the cavalletti and only raise poles on the inside.

### Your Horse Has Mastered This Exercise—What's Next?
➡ Make sure you and your horse both feel comfortable with this exercise in both directions. Then, I'd suggest you take a break before moving on to the next exercise.

## 8.5 Cavalletti in Gradual Stages

*Now we will continue with cavalletti set up in* **stages**. *Set up the cavalletti as shown in the arena diagram.*

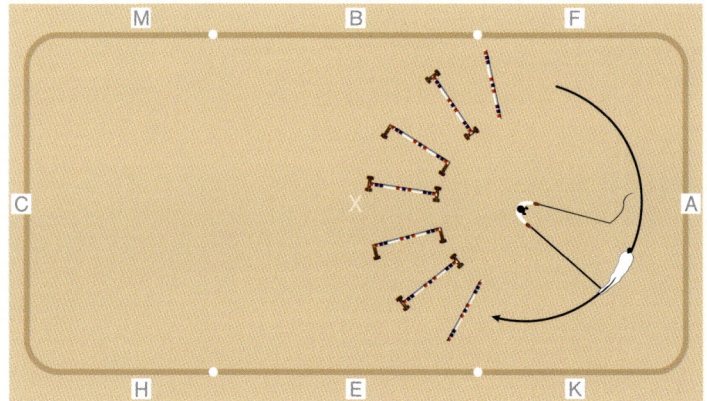

➡ **Depending on how you change the setup, you can train for various goals.**

Start by longeing your horse next to the cavalletti and poles until he finds a steady rhythm. Now let him canter over the cavalletti and poles. It's important for the horse to canter over the center of the cavalletti.

➡ *Important: Only use side-reins after consulting your trainer! When in doubt, don't use them.*

Prerequisites for this exercise include all earlier exercises in this chapter, in addition to all exercises in chapter 4.

> ### Solutions to Common Problems
>
> **"My horse comes more and more on the forehand, and either starts running after the last pole or changes to a cross canter."**
> - Your horse has not found his balance yet. He's trying to regain balance. This exercise is still too challenging for your horse. Backtrack several exercises. Balance is essential to achieve rhythm and relaxation. Always be mindful of achieving balance.

### Your Horse Has Mastered This Exercise—What's Next?
- Make sure you and your horse both feel comfortable with this exercise in both directions. Be proud of yourselves! Then, I'd suggest you take a break before moving on to the next chapter.

# 9. CANTER POLES ON BENDING LINES

Canter poles on bending lines are easier to ride than canter poles on straight lines. A basic requirement is a following seat in order to stay balanced when the horse's movement is still uneven in the beginning. The correct aids are essential, too. See *Canter Aids on Bending Lines* (p. 136).

Most rider-and-horse pairs have a preferred direction of canter. This goes back to the natural crookedness of horse and rider. Despite having a favored side, you should make sure to train both directions evenly to develop straightness and symmetry in musculature.

In addition, it's important to always aim at the center of the poles; otherwise, the distances will be too short or too long. The exercises in this chapter can be trained under saddle or on the longe line.

Forgo the half-seat or two-point position, if possible, since a correct framing of the horse is very important and not always possible in jumping seat position. For young horses, the half-seat position can be very helpful, but all workout exercises in this chapter are meant for older, well-trained horses.

Workouts on bending lines allow for the forehand and hind end to synchronize, and for the forehand to adjust to the hind end of the horse. As a prerequisite, it's especially important to have mastered bending lines in the walk and trot.

Along with difficulties that may arise from the exercises themselves, you may observe, among other things, a crookedness that makes itself apparent in a slightly travers-like canter, with the hind end moving slightly to the inside of the forehand. Don't try to correct the hind end; instead, adjust the forehand to the hind end, correcting the forehand to the inside so the hind end and forehand move in a straight line. This can be achieved by riding shoulder fore or shoulder-in. Often, this problem is more prevalent on the "hollow side" of your horse, or is caused by incorrect use of the outside rein. An exercise positioning your horse to the outside can be helpful in straightening your horse.

On the "non-hollow" side, the forehand may shift to the inside. The horse will canter too far in with both forehand and hind end. Here, too, it's not advisable to shift the hind end to the inside. To the contrary—always adjust the forehand to the hind end. Move the forehand to the outside. For more on this, see *The Correct Bend* (p. 13).

The pole workout can only begin after these difficulties have been solved without involving poles.

9. Canter Poles on Bending Lines

Here, the distance between the poles is too big. The horse has to dive over the poles. In order to regain balance, he transitions to cross canter. You can recognize this when looking at the hind legs.

Here, the horse is too close to the first pole. As a result, the following poles will also be approached incorrectly. This leads to tension in the horse and to a tense canter. The flow of the movement is interrupted.

If the distance is too short, one pair of legs may end up splitting. In addition, the risk of injury is raised, as the horse could step on the pole.

Here, you can see the clear separation of the front legs.

Since the distance to the first pole was too big, the horse had to dive over the pole. Therefore, the distances that follow in the rest of this line of poles will be incorrect.

Here, the ridden line is incorrect. The horse loses his balance and breaks to a trot to regain it.

# SIDE NOTE: CANTER AIDS ON BENDING LINES

**Weight Aids:**

On the bending line, the rider will always use the one-sided weight aid (inside seat bone).

**Leg Aids:**

The inside leg actively supports a forward canter and helps the forehand to freely canter uphill. The outside leg is passively positioned farther back for the canter depart, and can move back to its normal position while supporting the ridden line.

**Rein Aids:**

On a bending line, the inside rein is always the positioning rein (giving and taking). By staying constant, the outside rein supports the horse's movement on the correct lines.

To create a correct and even canter, the rider must sit in every canter stride toward the outside rein—that is, the rider's hips will be moved forward by the horse, shortening the distance between the hip and the outside hand of the rider. At the same time, the inside leg should support the forward movement, and the inside hand should give, allowing the horse to open his inside, move his shoulder forward and upward, and lengthen the time he is supporting himself on one leg. Review *Half-Halts and Full Halts* (p. 107).

## 9.1 The Canter Square

*Before you begin with the pole workout on the bending line, you can start in small steps. Position 4 poles, spaced evenly apart, on the second or third track of the 20-meter circle.*

➡ ***You can use cavalletti instead of poles. But start on the lowest setting.***

## 9. Canter Poles on Bending Lines

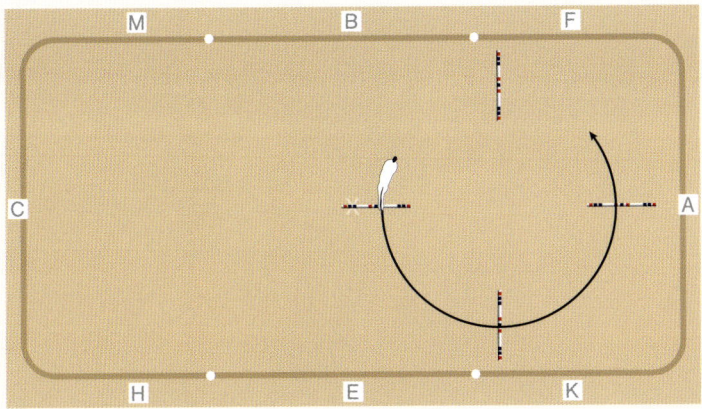

Set up your canter on the 20-meter circle. As soon as your horse is on the aids, ride your circle smaller so you go over the center of the poles. Count in your head in order to achieve an even tempo. For example: "1, 2, 3, jump." (At "jump," you should canter over the pole). As soon as your horse finds an even tempo and canters over the poles in a relaxed manner, end the exercise with extensive praise. Practice this exercise in both directions.

Just like the last few chapters, this exercise is geared more toward the rider's improved coordination than toward the horse developing musculature. Please remember this before you continue with the following exercises, which are more difficult. This exercise, even if it seems simple, needs to be fully mastered before you tackle more challenging exercises.

### Solutions to Common Problems

**"My horse falls in and the bending line gets smaller and smaller."**
- Ride this exercise like a square. Your horse has shortened musculature, and is therefore crooked. Make sure to sit on the inside seat bone without turning the upper body to the inside.
- Other problems with your seat could be the cause. Remember, the contact on the inside rein has to be a give-and-take, never a constant contact.

**"My horse falls to the outside and the circle gets bigger and bigger."**
- Here, again, crookedness is likely the cause. The source could be the horse or the rider. Frame your horse clearly with a quiet, constant contact. While counting, ride straight on "1," turn on "2," go straight on "3," and then "jump" over the pole.

On the bending line, be aware of your shoulders; you need to keep your inside shoulder level with your outside shoulder to avoid folding at the hip.

### Your Horse Has Mastered This Exercise—What's Next?

➡ Make sure you and your horse both feel comfortable with this exercise in both directions. Then, I'd suggest you take a break before moving on to the next exercise.

## 9.2 The Canter Quartet

*Next, position the 4 poles in a row on the circle line (second track). Now the correct and even canter stride will be combined with the correct bend.*

➡ **Start by placing the poles about 20 feet (6 meters) apart on the circle line. This will be easier for some.**

Set up your canter on the 20-meter circle. As soon as your horse is on the aids, ride your circle smaller so you go over the center of the poles. Count in your head in order to achieve an even tempo: "1, 2, 3, jump." (At "jump," you should canter over the pole.)

## 9. Canter Poles on Bending Lines

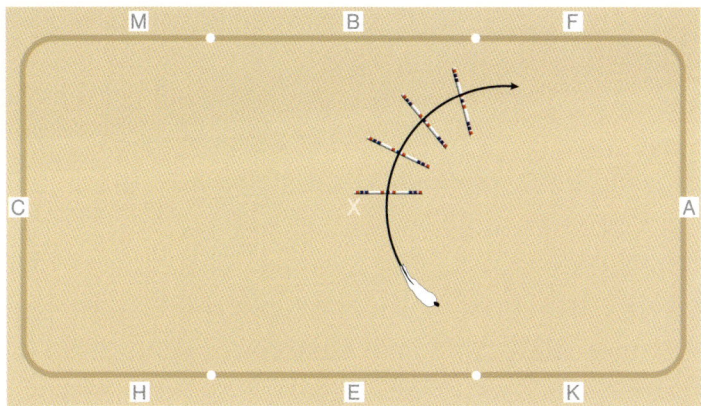

To achieve a correct bending line before, over, and after the poles, stay on a smaller circle until your horse canters fluidly and correctly over the poles and his rhythm stays the same before and after the poles. Praise your horse thoroughly, and allow for a walk break. Then continue in the other direction. You can build on this exercise by adding more poles.

With young horses, half seat can be helpful, but keep your horse in a good frame to avoid him speeding up over the poles, and to support his balance.

> ### Solutions to Common Problems
>
> **"My horse always speeds up before and over the poles."**
> - Prepare your horse for the poles with half halts.
> - Ride each canter stride as if it were the first one, and sit firmly toward the outside rein.

**Your Horse Has Mastered This Exercise—What's Next?**
➡ I recommend that you continue, after a break, with the next couple of exercises.

# 9.3 Abs, Legs, Butt

*Now we're getting serious, and the real workout begins! You're already familiar with this setup, but this time the whole exercise will be ridden in canter. Position 8 poles on the circle line. Raise 4 poles at the inside end and 4 poles at the outside end, so every other pole is raised on the right end and the rest are raised at the left end. Use the third track.*

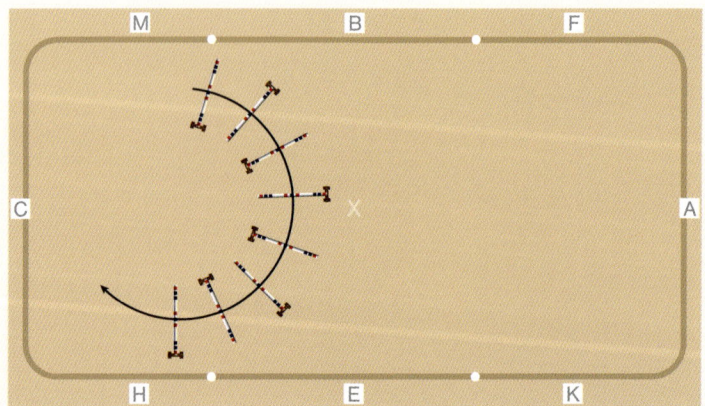

➡ *Avoid diving over the first pole. Choose your line correctly!*

## 9. Canter Poles on Bending Lines

Repeat this exercise over a longer period of time before moving on to the next exercise. Focus on suppling the horse evenly in both directions.

### Which Exercises Should You Have Mastered Before Starting This Exercise?
- The previous exercises in this chapter.
- The exercises in chapters 4 and 8.

### Solutions to Common Problems

- Most of the problems that could occur have already been addressed in previous exercises and chapters.

### Your Horse Has Mastered This Exercise—What's Next?
➡ I recommend you continue, after a break, with the next exercise, for suppling, or continue onward directly to a more difficult workout with Exercise 9.5 (p. 138).
➡ If Exercises 9.4 and 9.5 are too challenging, you can start chapter 10.

You can also raise every other pole on both sides.

## 9.4 Interplay

*Suppling and change are the focus here. This exercise develops the entire musculature in the canter on the bending line, and also the flying lead change.*

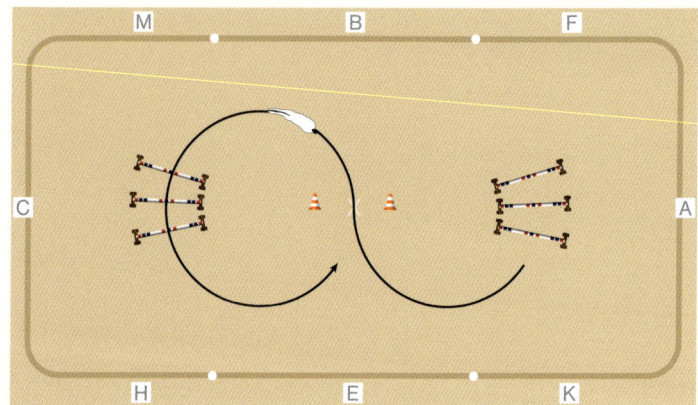

➡ **You can raise the cavalletti, depending on the level of difficulty you want.**

Set up the poles as shown in the diagram. Now begin in one direction in the canter. Ride over the cavalletti on the bending line until your horse canters over the cavalletti correctly and remains relaxed. Now add a simple lead change between the cones. Pick up the canter again and practice in the new direction. Once both directions are equally comfortable, you can replace the simple lead change with a flying lead change. A pole between the cones can help some horses achieve the flying change with more fluidity.

### Which Exercises Should You Have Mastered Before Starting This Exercise?
- The flying lead change.
- Exercise 9.3 (p. 134).

### Your Horse Has Mastered This Exercise—What's Next?
➡ I recommend you continue, after a break, with the following:
➡ If you're ready, try the next exercise.
➡ You can also move ahead to chapter 10.
➡ Any combination exercise from chapter 7 would also be a good idea.

9. Canter Poles on Bending Lines

Before initiating a lead change, the rider should look in the new direction and ride straight for at least 2–3 canter strides.

# 9.5 Infinity Loop at Canter

*This exercise requires not just a high level of muscle strength, but also endurance and coordination. For this exercise, you can spread the poles out evenly around the whole circle. Use the second or third track. You can raise some of the poles—but this also means raising the level of difficulty. Leave an opening at X so you can easily enter and exit at any time.*

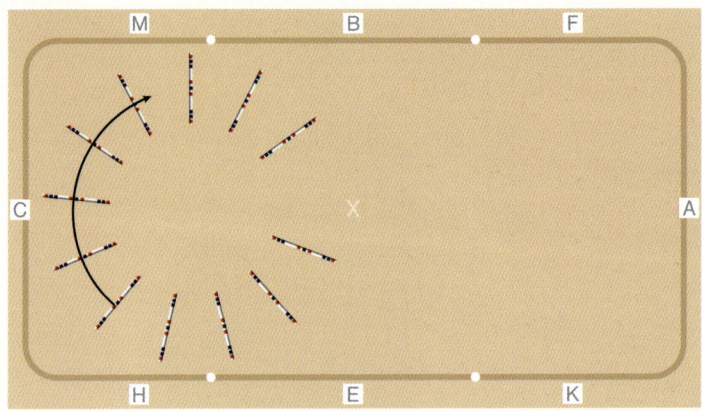

➡ **Stay calm and keep your body engaged. In order to achieve symmetry between both sides, the "weaker" side should be trained more.**

You're already familiar with this exercise in the trot. But in the canter, it can be intimidating for some riders—it's one of the most challenging exercises in this book. However, it's also one of the most effective! Canter your horse on the 20-meter circle (first track) until your tempo is even and your horse is on your aids. Now spiral in until you enter the poles at X. Stay calm and support your horse in every canter stride. Frame your horse well so you cross over the center of each pole. Ride each canter stride as if it were the first one. Keep your body engaged. End the exercise as soon as your horse canters calmly and evenly over the poles. Build in breaks for your horse. And please remember to practice in both directions.

9. Canter Poles on Bending Lines

Rider and horse are still a little tense. In this case, don't add any raised cavalletti. Keep a quiet seat and help your horse maintain his balance in each canter stride with half-halts.

## Solutions to Common Problems

**You are a bit in awe of this exercise and tense up before and during the exercise.**
- You should be very secure in your canter work. If you are insecure, start in the trot. You can also introduce your horse to this exercise on the longe line.

**Your horse speeds up.**
- Pay attention to the correct distances and support your horse in each canter stride.

**The horse falls to the outside, and the distances don't work anymore.**
- Frame your horse correctly. Focus on the outside aids. In addition, you can add visual support by placing cones in the outer third of the spaces between the poles.

### Your Horse Has Mastered This Exercise—What's Next?
⇒ I'm impressed—this exercise was one of the most difficult ones in this book! Have you already tried raising the poles? This will raise the level of difficulty even more.

⇒ If you haven't tried any exercises from chapter 10 yet, I recommend you move on to it now.

# 10. CANTER POLES ON STRAIGHT LINES

# 10. Canter Poles on Straight Lines

For many riders, cantering over poles set in a straight line is a huge challenge, since many horses get quick on the straight line and don't remain correctly on the aids. It's very important for the distances between poles to be adjusted precisely to the individual horse's canter stride. Many horses lengthen themselves over the pole or cavalletti and dive over them, and then the following distances don't work anymore. Riding 8-meter circles before and after the poles can help bring the horse back on the aids.

Here, too, daily or near-daily training is necessary to develop the musculature of the horse where it is lacking.

➡ **Always start with a few poles and broaden the exercise only after your horse has mastered the workouts. Too many poles overwhelm not just the horse but also the rider.**

Many riders prefer a horse positioned slightly to the inside, because he will stay on the aids and be less likely to get tense through the neck. If you choose this aid, make sure your reins stay soft, and position the horse less and less over time so his musculature can develop correctly.

Most of the difficulties that arise when working over poles in the canter are caused by a lack of coordination between the horse's centers of movement. Let your trainer help you ensure your horse is using his centers of movement correctly and therefore is on the aids.

If your horse is on the aids before the poles, but not at all while he is over the poles, he's mostly lacking balance. This means your horse wasn't truly on the aids before the poles, either. Please read *Positive Tension* (p. 27) very closely. An experienced trainer can help you with this problem as well.

## 10.1 The Canter Trio

*For the first step of your canter workout, start by setting up 3 poles on the third track of the arena.*

➡ **Look right in front of the first pole in order to determine whether your rhythm is correct for the distances between the poles.**

# POLE WORK FOR DRESSAGE RIDERS

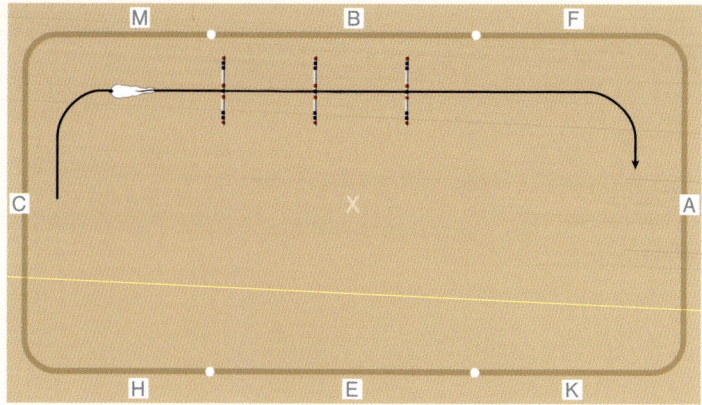

*If you aren't sure, ask a helper on the ground to watch while you ride along past the poles. Your helper can let you know whether your horse would have stepped correctly in between the poles.*

Canter around the whole arena on the third track. Choose an appropriate tempo. The tempo will vary depending on the level of training of your horse. The more experienced the horse, the more he will be able to collect himself, bending the hock joint and becoming more compact. The goal of the pole workout isn't to ride slowly, but to develop more carrying power, which will lead to higher and more ground-covering strides. Only then can shorter distances between the poles be productive.

Look in between the poles while moving over them, and move with your horse. Imagine four poles, this way you and your horse will stay focused and avoid hitting the last pole.

## Solutions to Common Problems

**"My horse can't find the correct rhythm; we hit the poles, or the distances are incorrect."**
- Go back to Exercise 2.5 (p. 25).
- Place a helper in the arena to measure the correct distances between the poles and adjust them if necessary.
- Start by passing the poles on the outside. A helper can estimate the distances, and can help you to choose the correct distance between the poles.
- Maintain a clear frame to avoid lengthening strides on the straight lines and maintain a steady working canter.

## 10.2 The Canter Sextet

*The next step in your workout. Set up 6 poles, similar to the previous exercise, in a straight line. Please only add poles once your horse has mastered the previous exercise without touching any of the poles. This can occur within one training session, or it can take a few days. Don't overwhelm your horse with too many poles!*

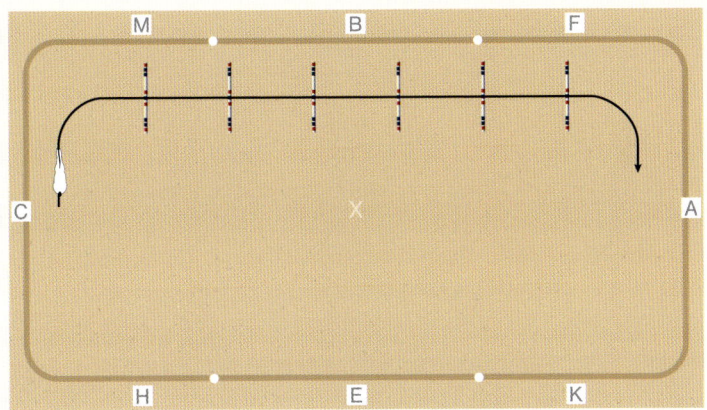

➡ *Shorten the canter before the first pole. Always remember to add one more stride, to avoid your horse having to dive over the first pole.*

Ride this exercise exactly like the previous one. Maintain the frame.

### Solutions to Common Problems

**"My horse masters 3 poles easily, but always hits a pole when riding over 6 poles."**
- Your horse needs to develop his musculature further. I recommend you go back to canter work on the longe line, or reduce the number of poles, and progress in small steps.

**We will continue with the long line of poles at the canter.**

POLE WORK FOR DRESSAGE RIDERS

## 10.3 The Long Line of Poles at Canter

The next step for your workout. Position up to 10 poles in a straight line on the third track. Please only add more poles once your horse isn't hitting any of the previous poles anymore. This can be achieved within one training session, or it can take a few days. Do not overwhelm your horse with too many poles! Take it easy.

➡ **Start by splitting the poles into 2 rows of 5 poles to allow for enough space to correct your horse.**

Use the whole arena in the canter. Frame your horse with every canter stride and prepare him for the poles with half halts. Look at the spaces between the poles. Your destination is not the end of the row, but each individual pole.

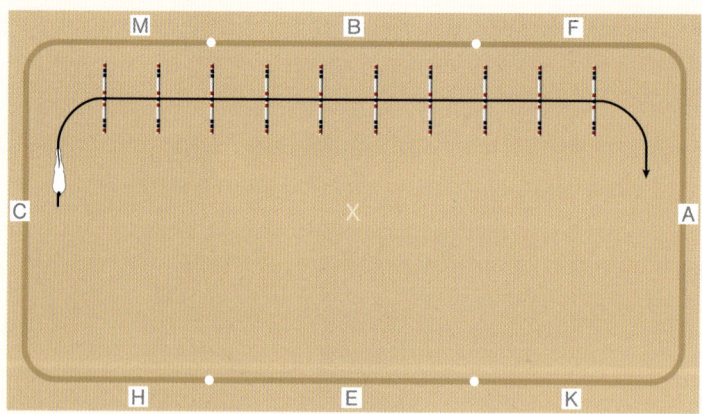

### Solutions to Common Problems

**"My horse speeds up over the poles."**
- Your horse isn't strong enough. As soon as he gets too fast, turn left or right, and ride a volte until your horse has regained his rhythm before either re-entering the row or starting over from the beginning. You can also start with just a few poles, and increase the number of poles slowly.

## 10. Canter Poles on Straight Lines

**"My horse refuses to go over the poles."**
- Did you overwhelm your horse? Or was there an incident the last time you worked over poles? If unevenness occurs after your horse steps on a pole, you should interrupt the training and call your vet. If he's physically sound, it's possible that he's lacking motivation for this exhausting work. Praise your horse every time he goes over the poles successfully.
- Build in more breaks, to allow your horse to recover from all this hard work. It's not for nothing that this kind of work is considered muscle training. Muscle soreness due to overdoing it can be very painful.

## Your Horse Has Mastered This Exercise—What's Next?
➡ I recommend you continue, after a break, with the next exercise.

Together, horse and rider are focusing on the next pole. Stay calm despite the number of poles. Maintain relaxation before the next row of poles. Shake out your wrists in the walk.

POLE WORK FOR DRESSAGE RIDERS

# 10.4 The Long Line of Poles, Raised

*Continue with coordination and concentration. First, we'll return to 3 poles, raising either one or both sides. Little by little, you can add more raised poles.*

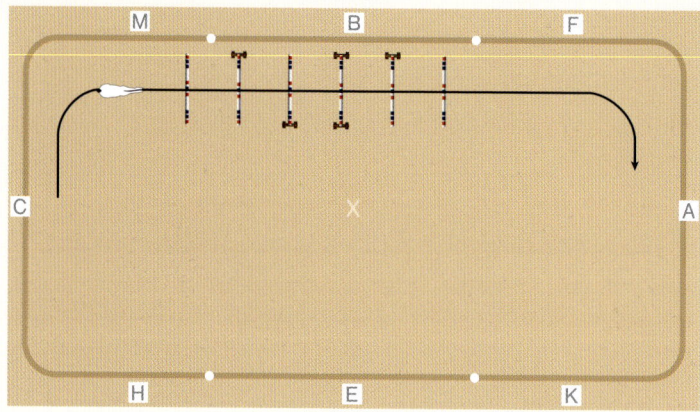

➡ **Position a helper in the arena who can add poles to the row.**

Set up the poles as indicated on the third track. Raise the poles, either alternating which end is raised or raising them on both sides.

Again, it will be important to ride over the center of the poles. Your horse has to lift his legs much higher than usual to avoid hitting the poles. You are strengthening the belly—and back—musculature, as well as the thigh musculature. This can be very challenging for inexperienced horses. Keep that in mind when repeating this exercise.

## Solutions to Common Problems

### "My horse always hits the poles."
- Practice with one pole so your horse learns to lift his legs higher to avoid hitting the pole. Praise your horse when he is successful.

## 10. Canter Poles on Straight Lines

**"My horse speeds up."**
- Build in a volte before and after the poles. Remember not to overwhelm your horse! If a horse speeds up, that usually indicates a lack of musculature.
- Ride each canter stride as if it were the first one. Support each canter stride with your aids and half-halts.

**"My horse mastered this exercise, but there is no improvement."**
- Your horse has developed strength, endurance, and coordination. Raise the level of difficulty and adjust the exercises to the level of training of your horse.

**"My horse makes an effort over the poles, but goes back to old patterns of movement afterwards."**
- Set up additional poles or cavalletti on the opposite long side. Many horses will only make an effort to change their patterns of movement if they really have to. Without the poles, they fall back into old patterns and have to be reminded by additional poles and cavalletti. After a few repetitions, their habits will begin to change.

### Your Horse Has Mastered This Exercise—What's Next?
⇒ I'm impressed! Your horse already has a strong musculature and is well-trained. But what about you? Are you ready for increased focus and strength? I recommend that you take at least a two-day break from pole work before you continue with the next exercise.

## 10.5 The Raised Diagonal

*Condition, coordination, and concentration. These "three Cs" will be the focus now. As indicated on the diagram, set up as many poles on the diagonal as you and your horse can manage. Only start this exercise once you and your horse have mastered Exercise 5.5 (p. 81) with a minimum of 8 poles.*

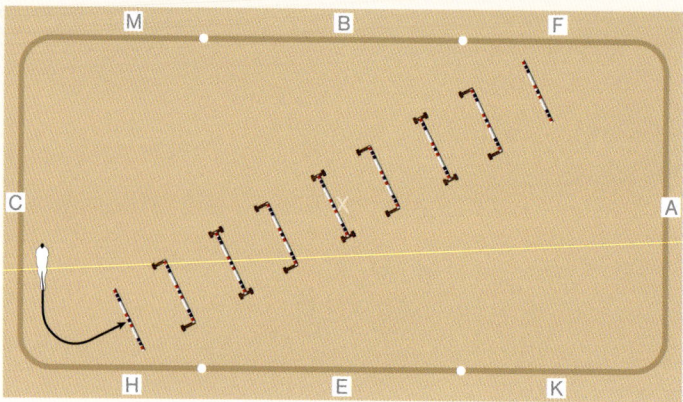

➡ *If you and your horse are pros, you can add "crooked" poles.*

Again, it's important to ride over the center of the poles. Your horse has to lift his legs much higher than usual to avoid hitting the poles. You are strengthening the belly—and back—musculature, as well as the thigh musculature. This can be very challenging for inexperienced horses. Remember that when repeating this exercise.

You can add a simple or flying lead change after the poles. A flying change within the poles is also possible, but only if horse and rider have completely mastered the flying change.

## Solutions to Common Problems

- As soon as problems arise, you should adjust the number of poles, lower any raised poles and work with fewer repetitions.

## Your Horse Has Mastered This Exercise—What's Next?

➡ You've done a fantastic job! Now you can get creative and adjust combination exercises so you and your horse can master them in the canter. Give your horse a two-day break first; go on a trail ride, or work in the outdoor arena.

➡ You can also start chapter 11, which incorporates changes of tempo in the walk and trot.

# 11. CHANGES IN TEMPO

Tempo changes are changes of tempo within a gait.

Tempo changes in the **walk:** collected walk, medium walk, free walk, and extended walk.
    In the **trot:** collected trot, working trot, medium trot, and extended trot.
    In the **canter:** collected canter, working canter, medium canter, and extended canter.

This chapter will deal with shortening and lengthening the strides and steps with the help of poles.
    In the collected gaits, the haunches have to rotate back and down, resulting in more active engagement of the hindquarters. In order for the hind end to reach under, the front has to create space: the front end turns forward and lifts up. As a result, the forehand is responsible for cadence. Cadence describes a slowing of the support phase of the leg, while the moving leg increases the space it covers. This is only possible if the horse has developed enough strength to avoid lowering during the support phase. If the forehand and haunches lower or sink, the steps get tense, and the parallel movement between forehand and haunches is broken or interrupted.
    It is very important to introduce collection and the lengthening of steps and strides in a playful manner, during the training of young or less experienced horses. Don't practice the following exercises continuously, but sprinkle them in from time to time.
    Before you start with the next exercises, make sure to re-read *Positive Tension* (p. 27) and *Half-Halts and Full Halts* (p. 107). Both are important for the following exercises.
    Preparatory exercises for the changes of tempo within the gaits are all lateral movements—shoulder-in and shoulder-fore—since they support an activation of the haunches and a forward and upward movement of the forehand. A brief transition to the walk can result in more activity in the haunches and a slight lift of the forehand. Only ride one or two steps in the walk, and then transition back to trot. A transition to a halt can have a similar effect. Immediately transition back to the trot to make this an effective exercise. You can find additional exercises in the book: *50 Arena Exercises and Patterns: Essential Schooling for English and Western Riders*.

## How to Avoid Tension

If tense steps occur again and again, the position of the forehand in relation to the haunches is incorrect.

The haunches don't lower and the forehand is not raised forward and upward. This pattern of movement needs to be corrected. In order to achieve engagement of the haunches, half-halts can help to interrupt the incorrect pattern. When encountering bigger mistakes, exercises like leg yields, shoulder-in, transitions from halt to trot, and transitions from rein-back to trot can help re-establish the correct pattern of movement.

As soon as the movement is correct and you're asking for collection again, it's important to prepare your horse with half-halts, in order to slowly increase the level of collection and keep the haunches active and engaged. Tense, short steps are mostly caused by too tight a rein and not enough activity in the haunches; collection is created only by shortening the rein and slowing down the tempo via the rein.

# 11.1 Lengthening the Stride

*This exercise will increase not only the amount of space your horse covers with each step but also the degree of relaxation in the musculature and engagement of the whole body.*

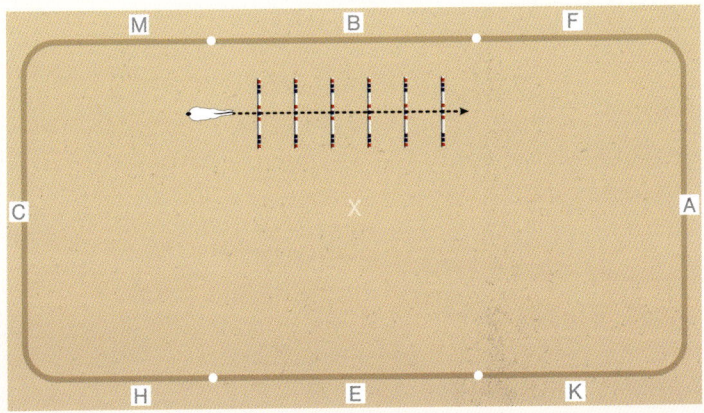

➡ *Position a helper in the arena who can help you adjust the distances between the poles.*

Improving the walk is an art. Influencing the walk negatively happens very quickly. Therefore, it's important to give the walk all the attention it deserves. Set up the poles as indicated in the diagram on the third track. Don't raise the poles at this point. Ride on as long a rein as possible around the whole arena. Let the horse's movement be absorbed by your body; your hips should move in the shape of a horizontal eight. Please don't actively push with your seat—instead, let yourself be carried. You can lengthen the forward swing of your hips, but don't exert any pressure. Help your horse lengthen his steps by giving with your right rein while the right front leg moves forward. And on the other side, as soon as the left front leg moves forward, give with your left rein.

## Solutions to Common Problems

### "My horse suddenly reverts to smaller steps."

- Often the issue here is actually with the rider, who tenses when applying the aids. As a result, the horse's musculature tightens and his steps get smaller. Focus on staying supple and relaxed.

The horse steps too close to the pole; either the distance between poles was too small or the approach to the first pole wasn't chosen correctly.

11. Changes in Tempo

The horse didn't step to the midpoint between the poles, so the distance to the next pole is too big. In this case, it would help to reduce the distance between the poles.

Here, the horse steps at the midpoint between the poles; the distance between the poles was chosen correctly.

POLE WORK FOR DRESSAGE RIDERS

> **"My horse trips, drags his feet, and hits the poles."**
> - The most common cause of this problem is that the horse is too heavy on the forehand. With the help of your trainer, analyze whether his centers of movement are coordinating correctly and whether the forehand is lowered. Read *Half-Halts and Full Halts* (p. 107) and *Positive Tension* (p. 27).

## 11.2 Shortening the Trot on a Bending Line

*This exercise helps keep the body engaged while shortening the steps.*

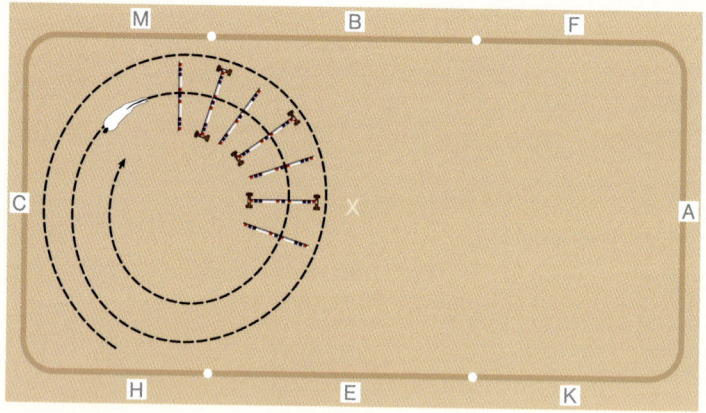

➡ **Position a helper in the arena who can adjust the distances between poles if necessary.**

Set up the poles along the line of a small circle, as indicated in the diagram. Ride a sitting trot on the circle line. Decrease the size of your circle until you are riding around the outside of the poles. Support your horse when the inside hind leg moves forward to ensure active engagement and increased carrying power for that leg. Frame your horse with your outside aids. Decrease the size of your circle even more, and ride over the poles once your horse's movements are light and flowing. Support your horse with half-halts and help him raise his forehand. Build in many breaks, in the form of exercises to loosen up your horse's musculature. Avoid any tensing of the musculature. Repeat this exercise several times.

# 11. Changes in Tempo

## Solutions to Common Problems

**"My horse falls to the outside and loses his rhythm."**
- Repeatedly build in shoulder-in and shoulder-fore.
- Remember your half-halts.
- Sit deeply into your horse.
- Make an effort to positively influence your horse through your seat.

## Your Horse Has Mastered This Exercise—What's Next?

➡ Wonderful work! Continue with the next exercise, or practice shortening the strides with a different exercise.

The hind end is clearly lowered by a deeper bend in the stifle. It's obvious that while the steps are shortened, the movement is flowing. The muscle chains are working well together, and the back is engaged and swinging. You can tell by the carriage of the tail.

POLE WORK FOR DRESSAGE RIDERS

## 11.3 Lengthening the Trot

*This exercise teaches the horse to expand his frame and cover more ground with each step.*

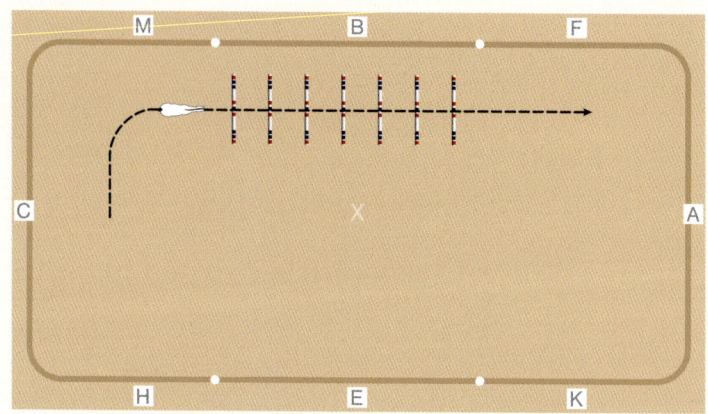

➡ **The more ground your horse covers with each step, the bigger the distances between your poles can be.**

Start by setting up the poles on the ground as shown in the diagram. Trot around the whole arena. Prepare your horse for expanding his frame in a playful manner by repeatedly riding shoulder-in to activate the hind end. Support your horse with half-halts and help him raise his forehand.

As soon as your horse reacts correctly and sensitively to your aids, you can let him expand his frame. Before you go over the poles, make sure you've checked the distance between your poles. Ride alongside the poles in extended trot and have a helper on the ground watch you and then adjust the poles, until your horse can easily cover the length of the distance where the poles are set up in extended trot, with good rhythm.

11. Changes in Tempo

Here, you can see how the horse is expanding his frame while going over the poles. For the horse to develop this expansion, it's paramount to increase the distance between the poles little by little.

The more ground your horse covers with each step, the wider the distances need to be between your poles. Build in breaks in the form of warm-up exercises. Avoid a stiffening of the musculature. Repeat this exercise multiple times.

Through this exercise, you can only develop the musculature to improve cadence and lengthening. It won't replace correct training of your horse, and it can't teach your horse the extended trot without a professional by your side.

### Solutions to Common Problems

**"My horse speeds up without expanding his frame."**
- Are you sure your horse has developed enough muscle to master this exercise? Make sure your horse is using his musculature correctly and is engaging his back. Repeat riding shoulder-in and shoulder-fore. Incorporate other lateral movements into your training program. Remember your half-halts.
- It may also be helpful to check and develop your horse's musculature further by going back to chapter 5 and using the exercises there to more thoroughly prepare your horse for this one.

### Your Horse Has Mastered This Exercise—What's Next?
➥ I recommend you move on to the next exercise, or—if the next exercise comes easily to you and your horse—to keep going, and review and solidify both by moving on to Exercise 11.5 (p. 161).

## 11.4 Collecting the Trot

*This exercise teaches the horse to shorten his steps and develop collection. The poles help to create cadence and increase weight carrying.*

➥ **Only raise the poles once your horse has developed the necessary musculature.**

## 11. Changes in Tempo

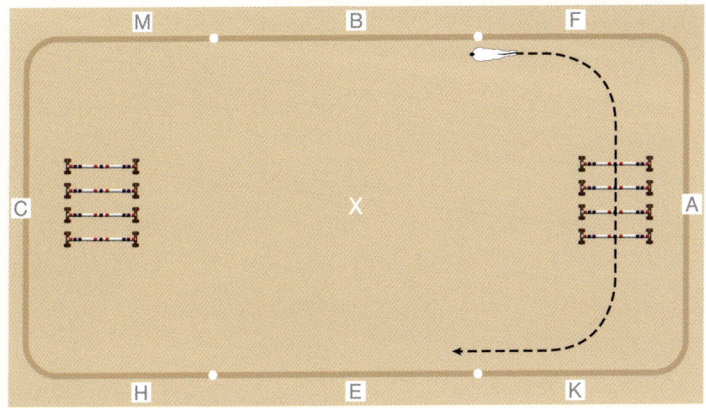

Set up the poles without raising them as indicated in the diagram. Work around the whole arena in a working trot. Repeatedly activate the haunches by riding shoulder-in. Support your horse with half-halts and help him to lift his forehand. Shorten the steps and ensure that your horse is on the aids before you ride over the poles. Support your horse over the poles. Little by little you can raise the poles. Make sure that your horse is strong enough. Build in breaks by riding warm-up exercises. Avoid a stiffening of the musculature. Repeat this exercise multiple times; remain playful and don't force anything. Your horse wants to be motivated and praise and petting will be helpful.

### Solutions to Common Problems

**"I have trouble with the collected trot."**
- Transition to the walk for 1–2 steps and then immediately go back to the trot. Half-halts should close the haunches and lift the forehand.

**"My horse hits the raised poles again and again."**
- Are you sure your horse is strong enough for this exercise? Take a step back and do this exercise with ground poles. Your horse may not have the muscle power to lower his haunches and bend his stifle and hock. Repeatedly ride shoulder-in and shoulder-fore while working on these exercises to activate the haunches. Remember your half-halts to lift the forehand.

# POLE WORK FOR DRESSAGE RIDERS

The positive tension is clearly visible in the horse and rider; it's time to decrease the distance between the poles a bit at a time.

Cadence and length of steps should stay the same without the poles.

11. Changes in Tempo

- Start slow. Give your horse enough time to develop his musculature. Increase the distance between the ground poles again and then decrease it gradually.

**Your Horse Has Mastered This Exercise—What's Next?**
➡ Wonderful work! Now continue with the final exercise in this book.

## 11.5 Changing the Trot Tempo across the Diagonal

*This exercise combines the shortening and lengthening of the steps from the last two exercises.*

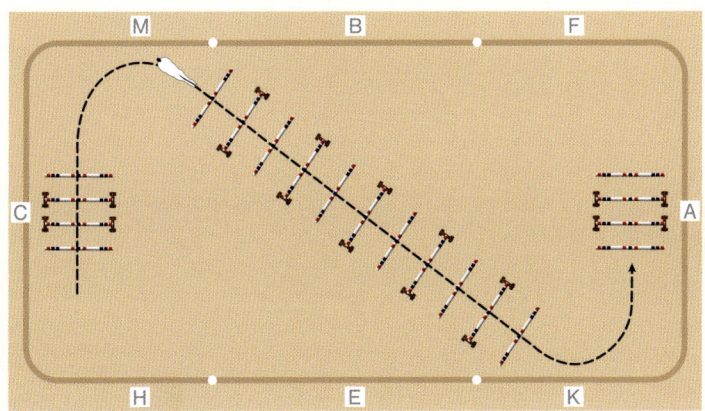

➡ *Before you start this exercise, you should have fully mastered the previous exercises in this chapter.*

Start by setting up the poles on the diagonal and the short side. The distances on the diagonal correspond to the distances in Exercise 11.3 (p. 156). The distances on the short side are the same as in Exercise 11.4 (p. 158). To increase the level of difficulty, the poles can be raised, as shown in the first diagram, or you can try the second version of the exercise, shown in the diagram below.

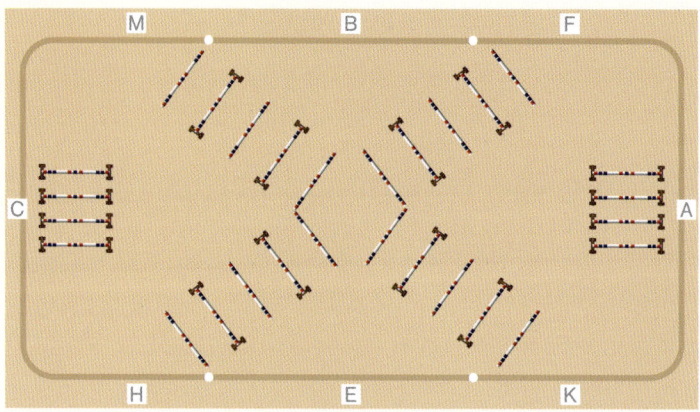

Here, by decreasing the distance between the poles, the horse's frame is shortened, the hind end is lowered, and the forehand is lifted.

11. Changes in Tempo

It requires strength from the rider to sit straight and supple while riding over the poles. Especially on the diagonal, it's easy to find yourself sitting crooked, as seen in this image. A helper on the ground can give you feedback and help you stay straight. Video and photos can also be helpful in identifying and correcting your own mistakes.

Now ride a change through the diagonal in the trot. Lengthen the steps, as in 11.3. Slow your tempo before you reach the rail. Support your horse and help him lift his forehand. Avoid blocking the flow of movement with either your seat or too much rein. Build in breaks by riding warm-up exercises. Avoid a stiffening of the musculature. Repeat this exercise multiple times. Remember to practice in both directions.

> **Solutions to Common Problems**
>
> **"My horse loses his rhythm and gets tense."**
> - Repeatedly build in shoulder-in and shoulder-fore.
> - Remember your half-halts.
> - Sit deeply into your horse.
> - Make an effort to positively influence your horse through your seat.
> - Accept help from a professional who can support you through these exercises.

### Your Horse Has Mastered All 55 Exercises, and His Musculature Is Perfect—What's Next?

➡ Splendid! I'm happy for you and your horse. I hope you can take away a lot from this book, and you're motivated to pursue new goals going forward.

# Acknowledgments

**Thank you**
… to all the physical therapists, osteopaths, and veterinarians, as well as to my farrier, all of whom supported me with their knowledge through the years to keep the horses I am responsible for in good health. All of you showed me that biomechanics are the basis for correct equestrianism, and helped me understand how to do my part as a trainer and rider toward maintaining my horses' health.

…to everybody who was willing, during the past few years, to support me in the practical application of my exercises.

…to my boyfriend. Thank you for always being there for me and supporting me in every possible way!

…to Dorothee Dumm, for the excellent interior graphic design. Thank you for your patience and your enthusiasm. I am looking forward to designing my next book with you!

…to Aline Arnold and the pony stallion Don Charlton, for your patience during the photo shoot. With your help, we were able to give life to the diagrams and present problems and their solutions.

…to Horst Streitferdt, Jasmin Ziegler, Sabine Kielmann, and Berit Wolf for the great photos, and to Claudia König for constructive conversations in the course of making this book a reality.

And, of course, I thank all my four-legged friends, who have taught me so much and turned me into the person I am today.

# INDEX

Page numbers in *italics* indicate illustrations.

Abdominal muscles
  exercises for, 81
  in muscle chains, 7–8
  strengthening, 124, 146
  tension in, 28
Abs, Legs, and Butt exercises
  basic setup, 55–56, *55*
  at canter, 134–35, *134–35*
  for riders, 66–67
Adding More Poles exercise, 38–39, *38*
Aids
  balance role, 141
  on bending lines, 14–16, 42
  in canter, 130
  diagonal, 14–16, 84
  in half-halts, 107–8
  at trot, 71–73, *72*
  in walk, 32
Alignment
  axial, 7, 16–19, 56–57, 128, 141, 150–51
  of rider with horse, 14
Approach, to pole setups, 47, 115, *129*
Arm position, *87*
Asymmetry. *See* Crookedness
Auxiliary reins, 48. *See also* Side reins
Axial alignment, 7, 16–19, 56–57, 128, 141, 150–51

Back
  of horse, 27, 81, 124, 146
  of rider, 66–67
Balance
  aids and, 141
  in canter, 126
  development of, 13
  improving with pole work, 5, 47
Base narrow alignment, *17*
Basic Setup exercise, 37–38, *37*
Bend
  aids in, 42, 130
  biomechanics of, 56–57, *58*
  correct, exercise for, 13–16
  on longe, *58*
  rider's shoulders and, *132*
  in trot, 13
Blocks (physical)
  in horse, 10, 53
  in rider, 36
Bodywork, 18, 52
Bracing, 27–28, *106*
Breaks, 95
Breathing, by horse, 28

Cadence, 150–51, 158
Canter. *See also* Canter exercises
  on bending lines, 128–30
  crookedness in, 128
  cross canter, 126, *129*
  longeing tips, 115, *116–17*
  preferred direction in, 128
  tempo changes in, 150–51
  uphill, *26*
Canter exercises
  on bending lines, 130–38
  on longe, 118–26
  pole spacing in, 141
  on straight lines, 141–48
  Abs, Legs, and Butt, 134–35
  Double In-Out, 121–23

How to Begin, 118–20
Infinity Loop, 138–39
Interplay, 136
Long Line, 144–45, *144*
Perfecting the Canter Rhythm, 25–26
Quartet, 132–33
Raised Diagonal, 147–48
Raised Long Line, 146–47
Sextet, 143
Square, 130–32
Tempo and Rhythm, 120–21
Trio, 141–42
Workout, 124–25
Canter Quartet exercise, 132–33, *133*
Canter Sextet exercise, 143, *143*
Canter Square exercise, 130–32, *131*
Canter Trio exercise, 141–42, *142*
Canter Workout exercise, 124–25, *125*
Carrying ability, 7, 14, 141, 158
Case study, 68, *69*
Cavalletti
    cautions regarding, 47
    exercises using, 121–26, 130–32, 136
Cavalletti in Gradual Stages exercise, 125–26, *125*
Change across the Long Diagonal exercise, 109–10, *109*
Change of direction exercises, 97–98, 109–13. *See also* Direction of travel
Changing Trot Tempo across the Diagonal exercise, 161–64, *161–63*
Chest
    alignment, 18
    in bending, 56–57
    lifting of, 27, 52–53
Chest axis, in axial alignment, 16
Chewing, of bit, 108
Circle with Eight exercise, 86–87, *86*

Circles
    pole spacing for, 115
    voltes, 24–25, 147
Collected gaits, 150–51, 158–61, *162*
Collecting the Trot exercise, 158–61, *159–60*
Combination patterns
    overview, 94–96
    Change across the Long Diagonal, 109–10
    Combo 1, 96–97
    Combo 2 with Change of Direction, 97–98
    Every Which Way, 102–3
    Figure Eight, 112–13
    Improving Transitions and Rhythm, 100
    Infinity Loop, 111–12
    Serpentines, 110–11
    Side and High, 101–2
    Simple Serpentine, 108–9
Combo 1 exercise, 96–97, *96*
Combo 2 with Change of Direction exercise, 97–98
Compensatory postures, 7, 61, 68
Concentration, developing, 5, 47, *59*, 79–80, 147–48
Conditioning
    exercises for, 63–66, 94, 138–39, 147–48
    pole work role, 115
    for riders, 66–67
Coordination
    of centers of movement, 7–8, 141
    exercises for, 63–66, 79–80, 138–39, 147–48
    improving with pole work, 5, 47
    of rider, 131
Corrective exercises
    theoretical basis for, 13–19, 27–28

Lifting the Leg with Correct Flexion, 23–24
Motivating the Horse, 19–20
Perfecting the Canter Rhythm, 24–26
Square of Cones, 22–23
Unconventional but Effective, 19–22

Crookedness
  at canter, 128
  case study, 68
  effects of, 56–57, 128, 131
  exercises for, 56–63, 85
  pole work caution, 11
  of poll, 18
  of rider, 32, *36*, *163*
Cross canter, 126, *129*
Croup, muscles of, 7

Diagonal aids, 14–16, 84
Diagonally positioned poles, 94
Diagonals, in posting trot, 104, 107
Diaphragm, 8, 28
Direction of travel, crookedness and, 56–57, 127. *See also* Falling in/out
Distances, estimating, 115, *116–17*, 119
Diving, at canter, 115, *129*, 134, 141, *143*
Dorsal muscle chain, 5, *6*
Double In-Out exercise, 121–23, *122–23*
Driving aids, *91*, 104

Endless Circle exercise, 63–66, *63–65*
"English trotting," 104
Every Which Way exercise, 102–3, *102–3*
Extended gaits, 150–51, 158
Eyes, of rider
  focus of, in pole work, 144, *145*
  posture and, *31*, 73, *75*
  seeing distances, 115, *116–17*, 119

Falling in/out
  biomechanics of, 56–57, 84
  pole workouts for, 58–63
  troubleshooting, 40, 85–86, 89, 95, 131
Fan exercises
  Finding Rhythm, 51–53, *51–52*
  at walk, 39–41, *40*
Fatigue, 61, 71
*50 Best Arena Exercises and Patterns* (Querbach), 13, 20, 22, 150
Figure Eight exercise, 112–13, *113*
Finding Rhythm exercise, 51–53, *51–52*
Finding the Way exercise, 49–51, *49–50*
Flying lead changes, 136, *137*, 148
Forehand
  alignment with hindquarters, 7, 16, 56–57, 128, 141, 150–51
  biomechanics of, 7–8, 27, 150–51
  elevation of, 115
  falling onto, 18, 52–53, 96, 126, 154
Forelegs, alignment of, *17*
Frame, of horse
  aids and, 84, 139, 154
  lengthening, 156, *157*, 158
  on longe, 48, 68, *117*
  shortening, 37, 72, *162*

Ground poles. *See* Poles
Gymnastic exercises, benefits of, 5

Habits of movement, 147
Half circle exercise, 20–22, *21*, 73
Half seat, 128, *133*
Half-halts, 86, 89, 107–8, 151, 158
Half-pass, 101
Halts, 107

Hands and hand position, 33, *34*
Head, of horse, 18, 27, 48, 52, 123
High Up exercises
   Part I, 90–91, *90–91*
   Part II, 91–92, *92*
Hindquarters
   activation of, 5, 28, 47–48, 57, 71
   alignment with forehand, 7, 56–57, 128, 141, 150–51
   biomechanics of, 7–8, 27
   engagement of, *82*, 115, 150–51, *155*
   exercises for, 19–23, *21*
   strengthening, 53, 124
Hips, of rider, *32*, 35–36, *132*
Hollow side, of horse, 57. *See also* Crookedness
Hooves, uneven wear on, 18
How to Begin canter exercise, 118–20, *118–20*

Iliosacral joint, 71
Improving Transitions and Rhythm exercise, 100, *100*
Impulsion, 22, 48, 58, 69
Infinity Loop exercise
   at canter, 138–39, *138–39*
   at trot, 111–12, *111*
Injuries, 7, 10, 16, 18, 45, 68
Inside-outside aids, 15–16, 18, 85, 130
Interplay exercise, 136, *136*

Jumping seat, 128

Lameness, 11, 18
Lateral movements, 150. *See also* specific movements
Lead changes, 136, *137*, 148
Leaning, by horse, 16

Leg aids
   alternating, 32–33
   on bending lines, 15
   in canter, 130
   in half-halts, 107
   in walk, 32–33
Leg axis, 16, 18
Leg yield, 101, 151
Legs
   activity of, 81, *82*, 91
   influence of posting on, 104
   strengthening, 124
Lengthening, of steps
   Lengthening the Stride, 151–54, *151–53*
   Lengthening the Trot, 156–58, *156–57*
   as tempo change, 150–51
Lifting technique, for people, 66–67
Lifting the Leg with Correct Flexion exercise, 24–25, *24*
Ligament injuries, 18
Light Workout exercise, 53–55, *54*
Line of Six exercise, 75–77, *76*
Long and low position, 33, *34*
Long Line exercises
   basic setup, 77–79, *77*
   with Angled Poles, 79–80, *79*
   at canter, 144–45, *144*
   Raised, 81–82, *81*
   Raised, in canter, 146–47, *146*
Longe exercises
   at canter, 118–26
   at trot, 45–67
   troubleshooting, 20
Longeing
   benefits of, 45
   at canter, tips for, 115–17
   equipment for, 47, 68

observation of horse on, 115, *116–17*
rider benefits, 33, 104
rings for, 121, 123
safety considerations, 47
*Losgelassenheit*, 27
Lumbar region
    blockages in, 28
    muscles of, 7, 8
Lumbosacral joint, 7, 53

Massage, 52, 53
Mirrors, horses as, 14
Motivating the Horse exercise, 19–20, *19*
Motivation, of horse, 13, 19, 39, 78, 145
Movement
    analysis of, 115
    centers of, 7–8, 28, 56–57, 71, 73, 141
    development of, 65
    patterns of, 147, 151
    phases of, *88*
    rider feel for, 73, 90, 107, 128
Muscles
    anatomical chains of, 5–7
    development of, 1, 39, 94, 128
    fatigue in, 145
    required for lengthening, 158

Neck, 7, 27, 38
Nuchal ligament, 5, 27

"On the aids," 28
Outside aids. *See* Inside-outside aids

Patience, of rider, 20
Patterns of movement, 147, 151
Pelvis, mobility of, 8, 14, 28, 56–57, 71
Perfecting the Canter Rhythm exercise, 25–26, *26*

Performance, as priority, 1
Physical conditioning, vs. training, 1
"Playing" with reins, 108
Pleasure riding, pitfalls of, 1
Pole spacing. *See also* Poles
    overview, *46*, 47
    for canter, *129*, 141, 142
    for longeing, 47
    for trot, 158, *162*
    for walk, 30, *30–31*, 37, *152–53*
Pole work
    benefits, 5, 8, *9–10*
    cautions regarding, 10–11
    for crookedness, 56–63
    demands on horse, 61
    horse's attitude toward, 19, 145
    phases of movement in, *88*
    progression criteria, *99*
    resistance to, 78
    session duration, 10
Poles. *See also* Pole spacing
    diagonally positioned, 94
    hitting of, 20, 39, 71, 146
    material for, 67
    raised, 45–46, 94–96
    safety considerations, 45–46, *129*
Poll, 16, 18, 84
Pony case study, 68, *69*
Positive tension
    in horse, 27–28, 73, 107–8
    in rider, 5, 73
Posting trot, *72*, 73, 104–7, *105–6*, 110
Preparatory exercises
    for changes of tempo, 150
    for pole work, 19–26
Pulling, by horse, 121
Pushing power, 7

Quartet exercises
   basic setup, 84–86, *85*
   in a Row, 89–90, *89*

Raise it Up Correctly exercise, 41–42, *41*
Raised Diagonal exercise, 147–48, *147*
Raised Fan exercise, 42–43, *42*
Raised pole guidelines, 94–95, *96*
Reflection, by rider, 1
Refusal to enter pole patterns, 145
Rehabilitation, 10
Rein aids
   on bending lines, 14–15
   in canter, 130
   correct use of, 73, *87*
   in half-halts, 107–8
   in walk, 33
Reins
   length of, 33
   "playing" with, 108
Relaxation, 108
Resistance, 78, 145
Rhythm
   development of, 5, 13, 47, 115
   exercises for, 20–22, 118–20
   maintaining, 54
   rider's sense of, 141
Rider position
   on bending lines, *132*
   centered, 35–36, *35–36*
   exercises for, 66–67
   faults in, *31*
   in lead changes, *137*
   in posting trot, 104, 105–6
Riding
   coordination in, 131
   correct vs. incorrect, 1, 7, 20
   over poles, *88*

Round pens, 121, 123
Rushing
   fitness and, 96
   in lengthening exercises, 158
   on straight lines, 141
   troubleshooting, 38, 124–25, 134, 144, 147

Saddle fit, 11
Seat. *See also* Weight aids
   centered, 35–36, *35–36*, 85
   in diagonal aids, 84
   exercises for, 67
   faults in, 22
   following with, 73, 90, 107, 128
   pushing with, 152
   straightness in, *163*
   tempo and, *75*
Self-carriage, 28, 107
Serpentines exercise, 110–11, *110*
Shortening the Trot on a Bending Line exercise, 154–55, *154–55*
Shoulder-fore, 128
Shoulder girdle, stabilizing, 56–57
Shoulder-in, 151, 159
Shoulders, of horse
   in bend, 14
   falling in/out on, 56–63, 84, 85–86
   falling onto, 18, 27
Shoulders, of rider, 14–15, *35–36*, *132*
Side and High exercise, 101–2, *101*
Side reins
   overview, 48
   adjustment of, *52*, *60*, *120*
   cautions regarding, 52–53, 123, 124
Simple lead changes, 136, *137*, 148
Simple Serpentine exercise, 108–9, *108*

Sitting trot, *72*, 73, *76*, 107, 154, *163*
Smiling, effects of, *76*
Speed, regulating. *See* Rushing; Tempo
Splitting the poles, at canter, 115, *129*
Square of Cones exercise, 22–23, *22*
Stance phase, of bend, 14
Stiff side, of horse, 57. *See also* Crookedness
Straightness, 56–63, 128. *See also* Crookedness
Strengthening exercises, 63–66, 138–39, 146–47
Suspension, moment of, 48, 75
Suspension bridge analogy, 28

Tail carriage, *80*, *88*, *155*
Tempo
    canter exercises for, 118–21
    changes in, 150–51, 161–64
    establishing, *54*
    lengthening exercises, 151–54, 156–58
    in longeing, 47
    maintaining, 47
    shortening exercises, 154–55, 158–61
    at walk, 37
Tempo and Rhythm exercise, 120–21, *120*
Tendons, injuries to, 16, 18
Tension. *See also* Positive tension
    avoiding, 151
    in axial misalignment, 18
    causes of, *129*
    effects of, 1, 28, 48
    loosening exercises, 30
    in rider, 152
    signs of, *80*, *88*, *106*
Theoretical knowledge, benefits of, 14–16
Thigh muscles, 7, 146
Thoracic spine, 7

Throughness, 20–22, 33
Trainers, 11
Training
    developing bend as, 14–15
    vs. physical conditioning, 1
    rider responsibilities in, 14
    variety in, 48
Transitions, 100, 107, 150–51
Trio exercise, 73–75, *74*
Tripping
    hitting poles, 20, 39, 71, 146
    horse's balance and, 154
Trot. *See also* Trot exercises
    aids in, 71–73, *72*
    bend in, 13
    phases of, 75
    posting, *72*, 73, 104–7, *105–6*, 110
    rider's feel for, 5
    sitting, *72*, 73, 107, 154, *163*
    tempo changes in, 150–51
Trot exercises
    on bending lines, 84–92
    benefits of, 47–48
    on circles/longe, 45–47
    on straight lines, 71–73
    Abs, Legs, and Butt, 55–56
    Change across the Long Diagonal, 109–10
    Changing Tempo across the Diagonal, 161–64
    Circle with Eight, 86–87
    Collecting, 158–61
    Combo 1, 96–97
    Combo 2 with Change of Direction, 97–98
    Endless Circle, 63–66
    Every Which Way, 102–3
    Figure Eight, 112–13

Finding Rhythm, 51–53, *51–52*
Finding the Way, 49–51
High Up, 90–92
Improving Transitions and Rhythm, 100
Infinity Loop, 111–12
Lengthening, 156–58
Light Workout, 53–55
Line of Six, 75–77
Long Line, 77–79
Long Line, Raised, 81–82
Long Line with Angled Poles, 79–80
Quartet, 84–86
Quartet in a Row, 89–90
Serpentines, 110–11
Shortening on a Bending Line, 154–55
Side and High, 101–2
Simple Serpentine, 108–9
Trio, 73–75
Trunk
  of horse, 7
  of rider, 35
Twisted rein aid, 14
Two-point position, 128

Unconventional but Effective exercise, 20–22, *21*
Under saddle exercises
  on bending lines, 39–43, 84–92, 130–39, 154–55
  at canter, 25–26, 130–39
  combination patterns, 92–103, 108–13
  on straight lines, 37–39, 41–42, 73–82, 141–48, 151–54, 156–64
  at trot, 19–22, 73–82, 84–92, 154–64
  at walk, 22–25, 37–43, 151–54

Ventral muscle chain, 6, 7, 94
Voltes, 24–25, 147

Walk. *See also* Walk exercises
  aids in, 32
  improving, 151
  quality of, 30
  tempo changes in, 150–51
Walk exercises
  overview, 30
  pole spacing in, 37
  Adding More Poles, 38–39
  Basic Setup, 37–38
  Combo 2 with Change of Direction, 97–98
  Fan, 39–41
  Improving Transitions and Rhythm, 100
  Lengthening the Stride, 151–54
  Raise it Up Correctly, 41–42
  Raised Fan, 42–43
Warm-up, 104
Weight aids, 32, 84, 130
Well-being, of horse, 1

Young horses, 45, *65*, 128, *133*